HOW TO USE MINDFULNESS TO BE HAPPY

By Jerome Freedman, PhD, CMT

Author of *Cosmology and Buddhist Thought:
A Conversation with Neil deGrasse Tyson*

Copyright (c) 2022 Jerome Freedman, Ph. D.
ALL RIGHTS RESERVED
ISBN

Disclaimer:

This material is copyright(c) 1997 - 2023, by Dr. Jerome Freedman, Ph. D. All Rights Reserved. This document is meant to be a description of the author's experience and he in no way takes responsibility for the accuracy or completeness of any medical knowledge or advice. The author assumes no responsibility for choices made by any of the readers of this material.

The author is not a physician and makes no claims about the potential usefulness of the subject matter herein to have any medical benefit. Please check with your doctor if you find something interesting that you would like to try.

His primary purpose is to introduce you to the possibility of employing *Mindfulness Breaks* in your life for healing, connection and deep peace.

DEDICATION

How to Use Mindfulness to Be Happy is dedicated to my long time teacher, **Zen Master Thich Nhat Hanh** (Thay) who passed away on January 22, 2022 at the age of 95. He was the founder of many monasteries in the Plum Village Tradition.

I first met Thay at a small church in Berkeley, California in 1984. When he said, "If the West stops drinking alcohol by 50%, we could feed the whole world," I immediately recognized him as my teacher.

After he had a stroke in 2014, I recommended that he be treated by Dr. Quoc Vo and I think this is what gave us another seven years with Thay. Sister Chan Khong said to me on October 10, 2015 at the Nourse Theater in San Francisco, "80% of Thay's recovery can be attributed to Dr. Vo." She later acknowledged me at a sangha gathering at Marc Benioff's house for introducing Thay to Dr. Vo.

ACKNOWLEDGMENTS

The first acknowledgement goes out to my wife, Mala, my three children, Micah, Rachael and Jessica, their three spouses, Ashley, Mathis and Vincenzo and my granddaughter, Ada. My family has taught me how to cultivate joy and happiness and I love them all dearly. My son created the first cover design.

The second acknowledgement goes out to the people who joined one or more of the classes I taught between mid-February and mid-April in 2022 as part of the Mindfulness Meditation Teacher Certification Training (MMTCP) requirements for certification. These include Abigail, Goldie, Jessica, Linda D., Linda L., Rachael, Tamara, Vivian, Kushi, Diana, Mala, Mary, Mina and Mathis, among others. Thank you all for attending.

The third acknowledgement goes to Tara Brach, Jack Kornfield and Sounds True for making this course possible and accepting me as a student. Thank you, Jack and Tara. Thank you Sounds True.

Next, I want to acknowledge the support of my mentor in MMTCP, Eve Decker and my peer group: Beth, Mary, Evin, Maria and Keith. Your encouragement and support was truly meaningful. I especially want to thank Andrea Starn, Beth Brener and Lois Soloman for their kind endorsements. Lois also was a great help in editing the book. Thank you.

I also want to thank all the members of the Bay Area Meditators (BAM) sangha who reliably met every Wednesday morning at 7:00 AM Pacific time and supported me greatly. I so much enjoyed our in person gatherings and especially enjoyed our getting together for the final sessions in Healdsburg.

The MMTCP was so rich in optional affinity groups and I want to acknowledge the mentors who led them: Jill Satterfield and Deb Kerr for the People with Disabilities, Chronic Illness and Chronic Pain; Crystal Johnson, Kitsy Schoen and Sarah Emerson for the White Affinity Group; and the members of the Seniors, Advanced Practitioners Group and the Jews Group.

Finally, I want to thank Thich Nhat Hanh, Plum Village and the Order of Interbeing for training me so I could qualify for MMTCP.

ENDORSEMENTS

"Jerome Freedman is a respected presence in our Bay Area mindfulness community. His long standing, deep, and grounded practice are evident in his teaching and writing, and greatly valued within our teacher's sangha. He is also a wise, kind, and thoughtful spiritual friend, and I'm excited that he will be sharing these qualities with others in his upcoming book."
-- Andrea Starn, Psychotherapist and Mindfulness Meditation Teacher

In, How to Use Mindfulness to be Happy, Jerome Freedman takes this heart-felt wisdom teaching and skillfully guides his readers on an insightful, tender & personal journey towards greater mindfulness and happiness. One of profound friendliness, skillfulness & accessibility, Jerome weaves ancient teachings with practical neuroscience and outlines meditations that are understandable & immediately useable. I finished the book with a smile in my heart and confidence that anyone who reads it will be encouraged and inspired by Jerome's deep commitment and understanding of these great teachings and practices.
- Beth Brener, Psychotherapist and Mindfulness Meditation Teacher

"This book provides much-needed guidance for those seeking to start a meditation practice. I especially appreciated the personal anecdotes, which show how the practice aided Jerome's journey through bladder cancer. His suggestions are practical and applicable for beginners, and his doses of humor make the book a fun read."
- Lois Solomon, Journalist

CONTENTS

DEDICATION 3
ACKNOWLEDGMENTS 5
ENDORSEMENTS 7
CONTENTS 9
FOREWORD BY EVE DECKER, MUSICIAN AND DHARMA TEACHER 13
INTRODUCTION 15
    ANOTHER STORY 16
    PERSONAL WILL STORY ONE 17
    PERSONAL WILL STORY TWO 20
    PERSONAL WILL STORY THREE 21
    WHAT TO EXPECT 23
CHAPTER 1: INTRODUCTION TO MINDFULNESS 27
    INVOCATION 27
    INSPIRATION FOR OFFERING THIS BOOK 27
    WHAT IS MINDFULNESS? 29
    BENEFITS OF MINDFULNESS 33
    HOW TO PRACTICE MINDFULNESS 38
    YOUR FIRST MINDFULNESS MEDITATION PRACTICE 40
    THE PRACTICE OF MINDFULNESS OF BREATHING 42
    CHILDREN'S PRACTICE – PEBBLE MEDITATION 46
CHAPTER 2: WORKING WITH EMOTIONS 51
    HOW TO DEAL WITH AFFLICTED EMOTIONS 57
    Mind and Store Consciousness 57
    RAELI 58
    RAIN 59

- WORKING WITH THOUGHTS 61
- THE PRACTICE OF MINDFULNESS OF THOUGHTS AND EMOTIONS 64
  - CHILDREN'S PRACTICE 68
- CHAPTER 3: UNDERSTANDING HAPPINESS 71
  - MISCONCEPTIONS ABOUT HAPPINESS 72
  - WHAT IS BEHIND OUR MISCONCEPTIONS? 77
  - PRACTICE WITH MISWANTING 84
- CHAPTER 4: HAPPINESS FOR LIFE 87
  - HEDONIC ADAPTATION 87
  - NEGATIVE VISUALIZATION 90
  - MANAGING REFERENCE POINTS 91
  - CHARACTER STRENGTHS 91
  - SOCIAL CONNECTION 92
  - TIME AFFLUENCE 94
  - CONTROLLING OUR MINDS 95
  - PRACTICE WITH HAPPINESS FOR LIFE 97
  - THE GOAL SETTING PRACTICE 101
- CHAPTER 5: LOVING KINDNESS 105
  - THE FOUR DIVINE ABODES 105
  - LOVING KINDNESS 107
  - THE PRACTICE OF LOVING KINDNESS 113
  - LOVING KINDNESS PRACTICE 115
- CHAPTER 6: COMPASSION 119
  - SELF-COMPASSION 120
  - THE PRACTICE OF COMPASSION 122
  - COMPASSION PRACTICE 124
- CHAPTER 7: SYMPATHETIC JOY 129

THE PRACTICE OF SYMPATHETIC JOY	134
SYMPATHETIC JOY PRACTICE	135
CHAPTER 8: EQUANIMITY	139
THE PRACTICE OF EQUANIMITY	142
EQUANIMITY PRACTICE	144
CHAPTER 9: GRATITUDE AND GENEROSITY	147
ABOUT THE AUTHOR	163
ALSO BY DR. FREEDMAN...	ERROR! BOOKMARK NOT DEFINED.

FOREWORD BY EVE DECKER, MUSICIAN AND DHARMA TEACHER

Happiness is a universal human longing. But how do we find it? In **How to Use Mindfulness to be Happy**, Jerome Freedman explores time honored practices that can truly support greater levels of happiness. Jerome shares ancient wisdom stories, personal anecdotes, and modern neuroscience to help the reader feel the true potential for happiness in these 2,500-year-old practices. What a gift!

I met Jerome in February 2021. He was in one of the groups I was mentoring for the Mindfulness Meditation Teacher Certification Program, a two-year mindfulness teacher certification program led by wisdom teachers Jack Kornfield and Tara Brach.

Jerome's friendly and patient personality speaks to his years of practice, both formally and in daily life, with both mindfulness and the 'heart practices' he so skillfully teaches about – lovingkindness, compassion, appreciation, and equanimity. Jerome is a warm guide for his readers, offering many stories of his deliberate practices over many years on behalf of both for himself and his family, which have resulted in not only his own contentment, but the happiness and well-being of his three grown children and their families.

At the beginning of the second year of the Mindfulness Meditation Teacher Certification Program, all students are required to write curriculum for and teach two 'practicums', or classes. The topic for the first practicum is Introduction to Mindfulness. Students have more creative leeway with the content for the second practicum. Jerome was very clear – he wanted to share with others the practices that have contributed to his own happy and thriving family.

So, Jerome's second practicum was about 'how to use mindfulness to be happy'. The class was very successful, but because of the time limits of the class time, he couldn't include all of the teachings, practices, stories, and science that he had gathered. So, he decided to write this book.

You hold in your hands a very generous offering. A labor of

love and care from a person who has traveled in the trenches of life and knows what has supported his happy family, and his students and colleagues. Enjoy the teachings and personal testimonials, and try the practices Jerome suggests. You too can learn How to Use Mindfulness to Be Happy!
-Eve Decker
Buddhist Teacher, Coach, and Musician

INTRODUCTION

This book is a result of a series of teachings I offered between February and April in 2022 during the pandemic. I decided to write this book because the one hour classes did not allow me to cover all the material I had prepared to talk about. The story does not begin there. If you want to skip to the main content and jump right in to *How to Use Mindfulness to Be Happy*, be my guest!

We have to go all the way back to 2008 when I was ordained as a member of Thich Nhat Hanh's Order of Interbeing. This ordination authorized me to organize a *sangha*, a community of like-minded people who come together to share stories, talk and meditate. I founded the Mindfulness In Healing sangha on the summer solstice in 2009 and it continues today.

The initial members of the sangha were people like me who had been treated for cancer and other possibly life-threatening illnesses. We did not distinguish between patients and caregivers. We treated them all with grace, love and compassion. We were granted the privilege to meet at the Pine Street Clinic in San Anselmo, California, where the pioneering work on dogs sniffing cancer took place. During Covid, we meet online on Zoom.

I discovered an innate talent for creating meaningful guided meditations based on the stories we heard in sangha. These guided meditations seemed to help patients and caretakers, alike.

We continued this pattern for about five years at which time we were joined by members of another local sangha with a somewhat different agenda. The members of this joined sangha preferred a period of silent meditation with walking meditation when the weather permitted and what we call dharma sharing.

In dharma sharing, members are asked to bow in when they have something to share and bow out when they are done speaking. We hold whatever is heard in strict confidence and we agree to deep listening and loving speech.

Deep listening is listening with an open heart with your full attention to what is being said without planning what you are going to say when it is your turn to share. In loving speech, we speak from the heart of what is true for us at the moment we are speaking. We make sure what we say is relevant, kind and timely.

We do not comment on what others say without their explicit permission and we refrain from gossip.

Now according to the law of impermanence, everything changes, even our sangha. Until I began the teachings on *How to Use Mindfulness to Be Happy*, we would begin with an invocation, sit in silence for 30 minutes and then I would either offer a teaching or we would jump right into dharma sharing.

So what happened to inspire me to offer the teachings on *How to Use Mindfulness to Be Happy*? This is another story.

ANOTHER STORY

Covid hit in March of 2020 and I, being at great risk of catching it because of advanced stage kidney disease and the continued threat of the return of muscle invasive bladder cancer, had to take precautions not to be around any people who could even possibly infect me. Here I was, in my beautiful home in Marin County, California sitting on my easy couch watching too too much TV.

Then, an email came from the Enneagram Prison Project (EPP) in which they offered to teach *9 Prisons 1 Key (9P1K)*, the course they use with inmates in prisons in California, Minnesota, Texas, Belgium, France and other places on line on Zoom. I did not hesitate to sign up.

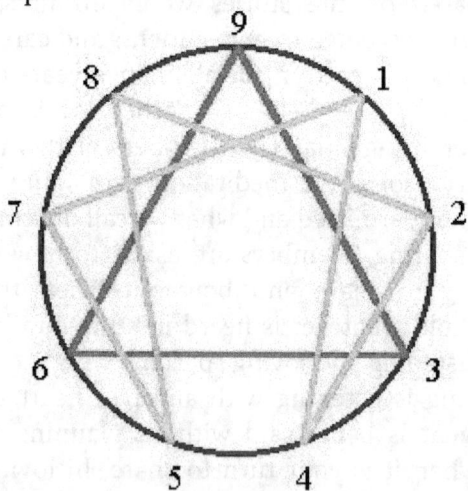

I first learned of the enneagram in 1970 or 1971 from Alice who showed me the full page announcement for the Arica 40 day training in Arica, Chile. The next summer, I met Rabbi Zalman Schachter in Rocky Mountain National Park. He led us to the Lama Foundation in New Mexico and then we met up again in Berkeley, California. It was there that he introduced me to Dr. Claudio Naranjo, a Chilean psychiatrist who had taken the 40 day Arica training and was beginning to integrate some psychology and science into the study of the Enneagram. In 1974, he taught his first class on the Enneagram in a beautiful home in Berkeley, California and I was there.

Fourteen years later, I began training in the Enneagram with Helen Palmer and Dr. David Daniels. These were the leading Enneagram teachers of that time as Helen's book; *The Enneagram* had just been published. In 1991 I was certified as an Enneagram teacher in what is now known as the Narrative Tradition with Helen and David.

Fast forward to 2022, and there I was, a total couch potato watching TV and the EEP announcement of *Nine Prisons One Key* caught my attention. The course was to be offered online with an online learning center to supplement in person Zoom classes with qualified instructors called guides.

It was during one of these online sessions that I came to understand that my experience of "personal will" was not unique and it was shared by other people of my type. What I mean by "personal will" is best explained by guess what, two more stories.

For more information about the Enneagram, visit enneagram-instrument.org.

PERSONAL WILL STORY ONE

In 1976, I was spending a lot of time with Gabrielle Roth, founder and author of *The Five Rhythms*. We were close friends and that February, we sponsored together an event at the Scottish Rite Memorial Temple in San Francisco attended by more than 200 people who danced and sang with Gabrielle. In May of that year, she invited me to join her at the Esalen retreat center in Big Sur, California in June as her assistant for a four or five day retreat. I was thrilled.

The day I was supposed to go to Esalan, my ex-wife, Linda,

informed me that my son, Micah, was in the hospital with a severe ache in his abdomen. I had had a hunch that something was wrong one day in the Arboretum in Golden Gate Park when he complained about a stomach ache. He was seven years old and loved to climb this beautiful cedar tree near where we were sitting when he told me.

On that fateful day, I had to cancel my plans to go with Gabrielle and head for the hospital. When I arrived, I was given the terrible news that Micah had a metastatic Wilm's tumor (a cancer of the kidney common in children) which had metastasized to his lungs.

Then, "personal will" kicked in and, while Micah was in surgery, I got on the phone and rallied support for him by connecting with alternative medicine practitioners who I knew. One thing led to another and I was directed to the Gladman Institute in Oakland, California. I was referred to Dr. Sheldon Ruderman, who played a major role in Micah's recovery.

This "personal will" led me to teach Micah how to use relaxation and visualization to get in touch with cancer. My then girlfriend, Bonita Clemens, and I would spend alternate nights in the hospital doing visualizations together by Micah's bedside. These visualizations came out of my training with Father Eli, and that's another story which you can read in *Mindfulness Breaks: Your Path to Awakening*, so I won't repeat it here. I am convinced that "personal will" was made possible because of what I learned from Father Eli and the training I received from him to teach his method.

There was no way to predict how well these practices would work. All I truly know is that when Micah got out of the hospital and began working with Dr. Ruderman using what we now call "mind stories," which are similar to the visualizations that I taught Micah and that Bonita and I practiced, he started getting better. The first time Dr. Ruderman saw Micah, he brought a bag of mini-bagels for him and this endeared Micah to Sheldon right away.

Micah was scheduled for 16 doses of chemotherapy as well as radiation. After two or three doses of chemo, Micah was so frail that we knew the chemo would kill him. So we stopped. Can you imagine how surprised we were when Dr. Burnip, Micah's oncologist, consented immediately to stopping the chemo? You will find out later just why he was so willing for us to do this and other alternative therapies.

Dr. Ruderman was invited to share his out-of-body experience with Leonard Nimoy and the In Search Of... (a long-running TV show on various extraordinary topics, 1976-1982) team. He said that he would only cooperate if they would also tell Micah's story as well. Sheldon and Micah were filmed at Linda's apartment in San Francisco. In the film, the conversation went like this:

> *Sheldon: When is your birthday again?*
> *Micah: January 29th.*
> *Sheldon: If we keep doing this and keep doing what the doctors tell you to do, it's going to be gone!*
> *Micah: Ok.*

Sheldon continued to do "mind stories" with Micah for many months. I believe that he was cured by his eighth birthday, and it is impossible to know exactly when or how he was cured.

When Micah was eleven, he was a vibrant, gifted child involved in gymnastics and the San Francisco Boys Chorus. Eventually, he had to choose whether to stay with gymnastics or go with the Boys Chorus because gymnastics was 10 miles north in San Rafael and the Boys Chorus was 10 miles south in San Francisco.

He was a happy kid by this time because of the nurturing of my second wife, Mala. We took him to see his surgeon for the last time when he was eleven. The surgeon asked if Mala was his mother and of course she replied that she was his step mother. I was there and I heard the doctor say, "We weren't saving many children back then. [1976] Your son made medical history by surviving the Wilm's tumor."

Micah went on to sing his way through and graduate from Stanford University. He is now 54. He has not had a single recurrence of the cancer. He lives near us with his wife of seven years and has a daughter, Ada who is now four. He was a VP in a publicly traded high tech company and very successful.

If you look back at all the causes and conditions that made Micah's recovery possible, I think you'll find that my "personal will" may have saved his life. Not many parents would put the life of their child on the line the way we did.

If you find this story hard to believe, please visit mindfulenssinhealing.org and watch the video.

PERSONAL WILL STORY TWO

This story begins on the night before the Super Bowl in 1997. That would be January 25, 1997. I was at a delayed Christmas party in Mill Valley and when I went to the bathroom, I noticed there was urine in my blood. I didn't even tell my wife about it. Instead, when we got home, I began doing research on blood in the urine. I found out that it is called hematuria.

Further research revealed that it could signify bladder cancer and I delved into the details about the disease. I spent the whole night investigating the causes and treatments for bladder cancer.

On Super Bowl Sunday morning, my wife took me to the on-call doctor for our then concierge doctor, Robert Belknap. He examined me and sent me off to the emergency room. It was remarkable how quickly Dr. Harry Neuwirth ushered me in to the exam room and admitted me to the hospital. I was scheduled for a transurethral resection of the bladder tumor (TURBT) which didn't take place until two days later because I wanted to talk to the anesthesiologist before the operation.

The operation was successful and I was invited back to see Dr. Neuwirth on Friday. By that time, I had done more research and knew I had some phase of bladder cancer and learned that it was the muscle invasive type. At the appointment, I pointed to a page I had printed out with the various stages of bladder cancer and pointed directly to what I thought I had. Dr. Neuwirth was blown away.

Dr. Neuwirth told us that my choices were a radical cystectomy (complete removal of the bladder, prostate and lymph nodes), radiation and chemotherapy.

That evening, we spoke with our friend, Dr. Sara Huang, a radiation oncologist and she told us about Dr. William U. Shipley at Massachusetts General Hospital and Harvard University Medical School. He was doing a clinical trial on a bladder sparing protocol. I placed a call to him. He called me back the next Saturday and agreed to share his protocol with my medical team.

It was at this very moment that "personal will" entered my mind and I knew I had to try to spare my bladder and other body parts. This was later confirmed with a consultation with Michael Broffman, a multi-faceted genius who founded the Pine Street Clinic in San Anselmo and who became my quarterback for all my years of living with or without cancer. His advice was to try the bladder sparing protocol and if necessary, the radical cystectomy could be done in the future.

The upshot of this story is that I still have my bladder and all my parts and there has been no cancer since 2018. Throughout the 27+ years, I have counseled cancer patients in general and bladder cancer patients in particular. I was unable to convince a single bladder cancer patient to try the bladder sparing protocol and I would say that 90% of them are no longer with us.

If you are interested in more details about my journey with cancer, may I suggest you read *Stop Cancer in its Tracks: How to Embrace Mindfulness In Healing*.

PERSONAL WILL STORY THREE

Hopefully, by now, you have learned the value of "personal will". The two "personal will" example stories were accompanied by mindfulness meditation practices such as sitting and walking meditation, "mind stories", exercise and what is called "conscious conduct" in playing tennis. These complimented my medical treatments which recurred about seven more times between 1997 and 2018.

So we return now to the summer of 2020 during one of the sessions of 9P1K. I was sitting there on zoom and another person was telling a "personal will" story. This taught me that "personal will" was a universal characteristic of my personality type as taught by studies in the enneagram. I suddenly became aware that I needed to find my voice and share my wisdom and understanding with a wider audience.

To this end, I watched a presentation by Tara Brach and Jack Kornfield about the Mindfulness Meditation Teacher Certification Training (MMTCP) and spoke at length with Jack about my intention. The next day, I think it was 9/11/2020, I asked Kaira Jewel Lingo, a dharma teacher and former nun with Zen Master Thich Nhat Hanh to refer me to the MMTCP. She had invited me to facilitate an online breakout room for Jewish students in the Plum Village tradition during the day long retreat that occurred the previous month. The following day, I applied and the day after, I was accepted.

In preparation for MMTCP, I took the Power of Awareness course online with Jack and Tara. This and other courses and online programs were constant companions for me before MMTCP began in February, 2021. It would be a two year investigation into what it takes to become a mindfulness meditation teacher, even though I was already teaching. I was excited, open and felt stronger than I had been since the first months of the pandemic.

When MMTCP began, I jumped right in. I watched the monthly videos, did the monthly readings, wrote in my journal, attended the live meetings with my peer group and mentor, and became involved with a wonderful and supportive group of MMTCP students all living in the Bay Area. I even connected strongly with students outside the Bay Area.

The program is so exciting that it opened up many new threads of exploration for me outside of MMTCP when my "homework" was finished. I had already been pursuing threads of climate justice, racial justice and physics. The program added threads of DEIA (Diversity, Equity, Inclusion and Accessibility), trauma and trauma sensitive mindfulness, neuroscience and the science of happiness.

The program also required us to teach two complete courses, one beginning mindfulness meditation course and one advanced in the second year. These courses provide the inspiration for this book.

Now you have the full story.

Ready? Let's begin!

WHAT TO EXPECT

My initial intent was to offer a class called *How to Use Mindfulness to Raise Happy Children,* and then I realized that it would not be approved by the MMTCP committee on practicum courses. So I changed the name and the scope to *How to Use Mindfulness to Be Happy,* which is obviously the title of this book. *How to Use Mindfulness to be Happy* is an introduction to mindfulness practices with an emphasis on fostering positive emotions and techniques for improving happiness and the quality of life. As a participant in reading this book, you will learn what mindfulness is all about and how mindfulness throughout the day will help you stay more present. This presence will enable you to be present with your children more effectively and allow them to experience happiness growing up.

Each chapter will conclude with a script for a guided meditation with a link to an audio version in most cases. These guided meditations will be useful for you to experience what the teachings in the chapter are all about.

Chapter 1: Introduction to Mindfulness

We will learn a simple mindfulness practice and understand how mindfulness can help us be more present. We will be encouraged to apply what we learn for at least 9 minutes a day to help develop the neural pathways for presence.

Chapter 2: Working with Emotions

We will continue with the simple mindfulness practice and learn how to deal with emotions. This is important to what follows in the next chapter.

Chapter 3: Understanding Happiness

We will learn why certain things that you think will make you happy really don't amount to much and why this is so. We will investigate misconceptions about happiness and why our intuitions about what will make us happy are wrong.

Chapter 4: Happiness for Life

We learn how to counteract the negative effects of our misconceptions about happiness. We will develop some positive practices for happiness and some of the teachings behind them.

Chapter 5: Loving Kindness

We will learn what loving kindness is and how to experience it for ourselves, loved ones and acquaintances. The practices that we do in this chapter will help you overcome anger and resentment. Zen Master Thich Nhat Hanh (Thay) said, "The essence of loving kindness is being able to offer happiness. You can be the sunshine for another person. You can't offer happiness until you have it for yourself."

Chapter 6: Compassion

We will investigate what compassion is and how it relates to loving kindness. We will also learn the importance of self-compassion. The practices you will learn will help you overcome cruelty. Thay said, "Compassion has the capacity to remove the suffering of others without expecting anything in return."

Chapter 7: Sympathetic Joy

We will inquire into the meaning and value of sympathetic joy and learn just how sympathetic joy will help you recognize when others are experiencing happiness or joy. The practices we do will help you to overcome hatred. Thay said, "Sympathetic joy arises when one rejoices over the happiness of others and wishes others well-being and success."

Chapter 8: Equanimity

We will determine how to set up the conditions for equanimity to arise in our life and how we can face life with balance. Also, we will explore how equanimity is related to non-attachment and inclusiveness. This practice helps us to overcome prejudice. Thay said, "Non-attachment is the way of looking at all things openly and equally. This is because that is. Myself and others are not separate. Do not reject one thing only to chase after another."

Chapter 9: Generosity and Gratitude

We will delve into the connection between generosity and gratitude and learn the value of both in order to be happy. We will examine what it means to have enough.

CHAPTER 1: INTRODUCTION TO MINDFULNESS

I want you to know that you are very welcome to join me in exploring *How to Use Mindfulness to Be Happy!* You belong here if you want to learn mindfulness and be happy. I welcome all racial identities, ethnicities, genders, sexualities, differing abilities, sadness, angers, confusions, doubts, joys, passions, biases and prejudices, regrets, tears, laughter and triumphs. When we feel welcome, we tend to pay more attention and be more present for whatever comes up.

I honor your commitment to want to learn about mindfulness and how to be happy, no matter what your circumstances are in life. My teacher, Zen Master Thich Nhat Hanh (Thay) always told us, "We have everything we need right now to be happy!"

INVOCATION

Before you begin, I invite you to put your book down, close your eyes, take a deep breath and feel how your body is connected through your chair, bed, couch or whatever to the earth. This grounding practice can help you get the most of the book.

We begin with the invocation...

> *This life is the gift of the whole universe –*
> *the earth, the sky and many generations.*
> *May we learn to live in mindfulness*
> *in order to enjoy the wonders of life and*
> *awaken from our illusion of separateness.*

INSPIRATION FOR OFFERING THIS BOOK

Now that you feel grounded I'd like to explain my motivation for the classes I taught and for the writing of this book. My life has been full of happiness and sorrow, success and failure, gain and loss, pleasure and pain, praise and blame – what are called the worldly winds. On the whole, however, I have been able to maintain a sense of happiness throughout because of the love in my life. Together with my wife since 1981, we raised three children who are now adults and married.

My son, Micah, as I told in the introduction, is a very successful graduate of Stanford University and was a VP in a publicly traded high-tech firm. He is now 53 and lives nearby with his wife and three year old daughter, Ada.

My two daughters, Rachael (40) and Jessica (38) both married Europeans. Rachael graduated with a degree in architecture and is now a very well respected yoga teacher and Ayurveda practitioner in San Francisco. She offers classes and workshops at places like Google. Her husband, Mathis, is a PhD from Germany and now works for Google. Rachael and Mathis are also pursuing coaching careers.

Jessica married an Italian named Vincenzo in 2016 and they live the happiest lives you can imagine in Barcelona. Jessica holds a master's degree from the University of Barcelona. Her Italian passport is waiting for her the next time she is in Italy. She has degrees in journalism, Spanish and masters in tourism and gastronomy. Vincenzo also has a master's degree in a similar field. They love to travel, eat good food, hang out with friends and will visit us soon.

The wonderful thing about these "children"- as they will always be my children – is that they all like each other and go on vacations together when Jessica and Vincenzo are in the US. They seem to get along better than I ever got along with my five siblings.

If you have read the introduction, you may recall that Micah was taught to use "mind stories" to cure his cancer. When the girls were born, I made sure they knew how to do the mind stories as well. I used to read them from Thich Nhat Hanh's book, *Old Path, White Clouds*. This book is the story of the life of the Buddha as seen through the eyes of a nine year old boy. It is over 500 pages. I would open the book to a random page and start reading whatever story appeared. They seemed to soak up the Buddha's wisdom without even trying. This was usually followed by a mind story and they would sleep quite well.

So you see, I have raised three happy children who have all gone on to have happy lives. Bringing them up in a house with Buddha pictures and statues all over the place may have had something to do with it. At least my own spiritual practice which began in 1968 with yoga and meditation has given me the presence to genuinely be present for my children.

This wasn't always the case for the first seven years of Micah's life. This led me to seek out the Zen teachings of Father Eli and move to San Francisco. Things settled down for me after Micah got out of the hospital and I was settled into an apartment across the street from the Arboretum in Golden Gate Park. I got a job at the Bank of America and made sure that there was a comfortable bed for Micah to sleep in when he was with me. Mind stories were my principle practice at that time. Then, Mala re-entered our lives.

I first met Mala in 1974 in a house in Berkeley, California where Ken Keyes was teaching. We passed each other on the steps and smiled at each other. There was no hint of any kind of relationship developing. We crossed paths a couple of times at the organic food coop on Ninth Avenue. She was living in the same neighborhood and was working at the Sunshine Juice Bar, an organic restaurant on Judah Street. I would often meet Micah's mother and boyfriend there with Micah because it was the easiest place for Micah to get some food that he liked. I guess that having one kidney caused him to be very picky about his food.

One time in 1977 or 1978, Mala told me that she was off to India and I invited her to get in touch with me when she got back so we could compare notes about India. The day she got back, a December day in 1978, we crossed paths again and agreed to meet that evening at the Japanese restaurant on 10th and Irving. After dinner, she needed a place to stay so I invited her into our little home.

Somehow, Micah immediately began to bond with Mala and she became a member of our household. We married on Valentine's Day in 1981 at the Ahwahnee hotel, Yosemite National Park. Micah was my best man. He was eleven by then. From then on, our lives got better and better.

WHAT IS MINDFULNESS?

Now that you have some background, let's look at what

mindfulness is. Mindfulness is bringing one's complete attention to the present experience on a moment-to-moment basis. Jon Kabat-Zinn, founder of Mindfulness Based Stress Reduction defines mindfulness as

> *"Mindfulness is paying attention in a particular way: on purpose, in the present moment, and nonjudgmentally, as if your life depended on it."*

I think we all have a problem with judging our experience. To illustrate this point, I'd like to share a story. It is about a Taoist farmer who was tilling his field with a strong, beautiful white horse and the help of his son. One of the villagers was passing by and said, "How lucky you are to possess such a strong horse to work in your fields and a son to help you."

The farmer said, "Please do not be so quick to judge. How can you tell that this is good luck?"

The next day the white horse jumped the fence and ran away. Back came the village people who said, "What hard luck for you. Your wonderful horse ran away. How will you work your fields?"

The farmer was not worried. He replied to them, "Here you go again with your judgments. How can you know this is bad luck? Why do you continue to judge?"

A week or so later, the white horse returned to the farmer bringing ten other beautiful and strong horses with him. And you can probably guess what the villagers had to say. "Such good luck! Now you have eleven strong and beautiful horses. You are the richest man in our territory."

The farmer once again scolded the villagers for their judging minds. The following day, his son tried to ride one of the new horses and fell off and broke his leg. Naturally, the villagers came back and said how unfortunate the farmer was to lose the help of his only son. Again, the farmer scolded the villagers about their judgements.

Within a few weeks, war came to the region and all the young men were conscripted into the army. The sad villagers came back to the farmer and said, "You are so lucky to have your son at home. All of our sons are in the army and subject to slaughter."

Naturally, the farmer said, "Please, friends, do not judge. There is no way of knowing what is to come next."

I'm telling this story because I, myself, am judging all the time. Did I have a good meditation or a bad meditation? Did I get a good night's sleep? Did I get a bad night's sleep? Did I have a good exercise in the morning, or did I skip it? Did I have a good breakfast? The whole thing is all about judgment. I find the more I pay attention to the fact that I'm judging, the more I can catch myself and be on top of it.

I heard this story in 1975 when I was in India. It had stuck in me and I try to think of it every time I judge myself or another. Please, watch how you judge other people and especially yourself! A lot of suffering can arise out of negative thoughts about judging ourselves.

Along these same lines, when our children were little, my wife used to say, "To desire what you don't have is to waste what you do have." This became our mantra when the kids got lost in wanting everything at Toys R Us and judgment about their lack of a doll or bike or anything else.

Mindfulness helps us recognize the fact that we are judging our experience. Once we recognize this and allow it to be present without judgment, we can learn to nurture our experience and drop the judging mind. We will return to this in a later chapter.

Mindfulness means bare attention to what is going on right now in the present moment without judgment. Sharon Salzberg, one of the original three teachers who brought mindfulness to America from India and Myanmar, says,

> Mindfulness allows us to watch our thoughts, see how one thought leads to the next, decide if we're heading toward an unhealthy path, and if so, let go and change directions.

I like to think that mindfulness is awareness and alertness to what is going on in the present moment **just as it is**. We may be having pleasant sensations, which are just fine, and we experience them in their fullness without getting attached or craving or grasping for more. We may be having unpleasant sensations, which are also fine, and we are experiencing them in their fullness without getting caught up in the story they are telling or trying to push them away. We may be having neutral sensations, which happens most of the time, and we simply stay with them in the here and in the now. Whether the sensations are positive, negative or neutral, they will all change in the blink of an eye or the sound of a car passing by or a white cloud disappearing from the sky. The thing is, they don't last. They are impermanent and this happens to us. It happens to animals, seasons, oceans, mountains, rivers and continents. "Even the sun will die," as Eckhart Tolle famously said.

Jack Kornfield, one of the other Buddhist teachers who brought mindfulness meditation from India and Myanmar, likes to say that mindfulness is loving attention or loving awareness. He defines it as,

> "...an attention that's focused on present experience and an ability to observe and be fully present for body, for mind, for spirit and the vastness of life."

Mindfulness has basically two parts: one is a kind, loving awareness in the present moment and the other is an appropriate response to the conditions that arise.

My teacher, Zen Master Thich Nhat Hanh (Thay) says,

> *Mindfulness is the energy that helps us recognize the conditions of happiness that are already present in our lives. You don't have to wait ten years to experience this happiness. It is present in every moment of your daily life. There are those of us who are alive but don't know it. But when you breathe in, and you are aware of your in-breath, you touch the miracle of being alive. That is why mindfulness is a source of happiness and joy.*
>
> *"To dwell in the here and now does not mean you never think about the past or responsibly plan for the future. The idea is simply not to allow yourself to get lost in regrets*

> about the past or worries about the future. If you are firmly grounded in the present moment, the past can be an object of inquiry, the object of your mindfulness and concentration. You can attain many insights by looking into the past. But you are still grounded in the present moment..."
> "Mindfulness helps you go home to the present. And every time you go there and recognize a condition of happiness that you have, happiness comes."

And elsewhere,

> "When we go home to ourselves with the energy of mindfulness, we're no longer afraid of being overwhelmed by the energy of suffering. Mindfulness gives us the strength to look deeply and give rise to understanding and compassion."
> "Mindfulness shows us what is happening in our bodies, our emotions, our minds, and in the world. Through mindfulness, we avoid harming ourselves and others."

BENEFITS OF MINDFULNESS

Now we can talk about some of the benefits of mindfulness. One of the main benefits that I have found is helping me to be present. This is the most beneficial benefit of mindfulness that I, myself, have personally experienced. I can now be present with my family, with my friends, with my students, without too much judgment. And this is a good feeling!

Meditation is not necessarily for relaxation, and it can be relaxing. It can be calming. It can put you at ease. It has this wonderful quality that you will enjoy your life so much more with mindfulness.

Other benefits include understanding the nature of the mind – how it goes on and on from one thing to another. As we recognize this, we can cultivate compassion for our thinking mind and get an understanding of human experience.

Scientific experiments have confirmed that cultivating

attention and mindfulness give rise to greater resilience, the ability to concentrate and physical healing. My more than twenty-five year history with muscle invasive bladder cancer is sure evidence of the effect of my practice on physical healing. Beginning with the decision to use a bladder sparing protocol (see the Introduction), and continuing on through many recurrences, my practice helped to keep me alive and present for whatever was happening in my treatment. Now I have been cancer free for four years.

Dr. Daniel Siegel, a psychiatrist and neuroscientist, reported additional scientific benefits in a talk I heard as follows:

> ... *your cardiovascular, heart rate, blood pressure, cholesterol levels are improved. Your stress levels, including stress hormones, are reduced. You are actually improving your immune system function, so you fight off infectious illnesses. You're reducing inflammation by altering the non-DNA molecules that sit on top of the DNA, called epigenetic regulators. .... you optimize the reduction of inflammation, and now you also optimize the level of an enzyme that repairs and maintains the ends of your chromosomes, called telomerase.*

Mindfulness practices help you begin to experience peace within you and around you. Peace may not come all at once, but if you practice for at least nine minutes a day for three weeks in a row without missing a day I bet you will find more peace in your life.

Next, you may experience your heart opening to the people you love and who love you and begin to enjoy the wonders of life around you. You may see more clearly how the earth we live on is really a wonderful place to be. You probably will find more enjoyment in flowers, birds, trees, animals, and other life forms, recognizing that they too want happiness and to avoid suffering.

Your own feelings about yourself may reach a point where you are happy most of the day. You may experience a glimpse of the beauty and radiance of your own true nature.

You may be able to answer such questions as, "Who am I", or "What is my purpose in life?" In any case, the increased knowledge of your inner self will inspire you to keep on practicing for many years to come.

Many practitioners find that their health improves drastically as stress is reduced or eliminated from their lives. In my way of thinking, stress is the extra suffering we put on ourselves over and above the challenges that life brings. Mindfulness practices are the path to lessening the hold of the stress of our addictions and bring about increased wellness.

Quite often, practitioners experience a degree of happiness far above their normal state. This happiness comes from the freedom experienced while sitting quietly and recognizing that one can be content with one's own life situation just as it is. This freedom provides an insight into taking life in the present moment, without putting anything extra on it in the way of stress or extra effort to get things accomplished.

Life seems to be experienced "in the now" – not just on the tennis court, for example, but also in playing, exercising, working, creating, loving, eating, sleeping, dreaming, and other aspects of the whole wondrous experience of living.

As you continue to practice, you may find that your addictions have less hold on your mind. Suppose you feel addicted to caffeine in one form or another, e. g., Starbucks or Peet's coffee, chocolate, TV shows, and the like. In the past, you would not stop a moment to think about getting that extra cup of coffee or having that additional piece of chocolate or watching that TV show. However, with mindfulness practices, you start to become aware of these kinds of urges as seeds before they reach the level of mind consciousness causing you to act impulsively. You then notice, "My little coffee addiction – I know you are there and I am here for you. Please remain a seed for a little while longer and I will take care of you."

A benefit that people experience out the gate is that of deep relaxation. Mindfulness practices bring on the relaxation response in most people, even the very first time they try it. The feeling of relaxation that comes with sitting silently can make you feel like you have slept peacefully for some length of time. You may come out of your session being quite refreshed and ready to take on your abundant life.

Another benefit that sitting quietly brings is the possibility of insight into various aspects of your life. Insight is the process of recognizing something important in just about any phase of existence. As you practice, sensations arise that give you a new understanding of your life situation.

Long time practitioners begin to notice a fondness and reverence for life. Aware of the suffering caused by the destruction of life, they commit themselves to cultivating compassion and finding ways to protect the lives of people, animals, plants and minerals. They also try to minimize the amount of killing in the world and are themselves dedicated not to kill, even a tiny spider, or to let others kill.

Also, long-time practitioners become aware of the challenges caused by exploitation, social injustice, stealing, and oppression, and they commit themselves to practicing generosity by sharing their time, energy, and material resources with those in need.

They cultivate loving kindness and compassion for all beings and respect their rights and property. Along the same lines, experienced practitioners regard the sanctity of sexual conduct of prime importance and experience sexual relationship in situations when there is love and a long-term commitment. They do everything possible to protect children from sexual abuse and try to keep couples and families together.

Experienced practitioners cultivate deep listening and loving speech. They listen with full attention and try not to judge what they hear. They speak their truth as much as possible in order to help resolve conflicts and protect their families and communities from harm.

Furthermore, experienced practitioners are mindful in what they consume. They avoid alcohol and other intoxicants and ensure their well-being by eating properly and not overspending.

They work to transform violence, fear, anger, and confusion in themselves and in their environment. There are several attitudes adopted by mindfulness practitioners that trigger skillful behavior when it comes to life situations. These qualities of the heart, as they are known, include generosity, morality, patience, and determination, among others. These qualities provide incentives for mindfulness in daily life.

The long term benefits of practice provide scaffolding for meeting the suffering of the world. For me, racial justice became a major concern. I signed up for many online Zoom meetings dealing with racism. In one of these meetings, sponsored by the Mind and Life Institute, founded by the Dalai Lama to explore the connection between science and Buddhism there was a presentation on Transformative Change: Where Research and Action in the World meet. The presenters were Doris F. Chang, PhD, Reggie Hubbard, Grant Jones, Shankari Goldstein, all BIPOC (Black, Indigenous, People of Color). I asked the final question about how to tell just how racist we are. The panel was intrigued by this question and there was no clear answer. Among the answers from all the panelists there was one particular answer that deeply touched me. Reggie Hubbard said,

> ...So compassion practice is key. The awareness that we're never going to [be free of racism]. Racism exists in black and brown cultures. "You're light skinned. No you're not!" All this stuff is everywhere. The term "high yellow." All this crazy stuff that has been visited upon all of us because of that. So we will never be cured of racism, writ large, as a structure. We can, however, be cured of our attachment to the norms through increasing awareness through contemplative practice.

Another concern that we can apply our mindfulness to is climate change. I have been involved with climate justice since about 2006 with Al Gore's *An Inconvenient Truth*. I was a founding member of the Earth Holder Sangha in 2014 and Buddhist Climate Action Network and in 2015. The former is part of the Plum Village tradition. I was invited to present at the first Earth Holder Retreat at the Deer Park Monastery in Escondido, California in 2016. You can watch the presentation on my YouTube channel.

At the time of this writing, the world was still immersed in the most devastating pandemic that humans have ever seen. This led to the deaths of over six million people worldwide. So far (knock on wood) the only way it has affected me is through three vaccinations. Luckily, no one close to me died and two of my brothers recovered nicely from a mild case.

My approach to the pandemic was simply to be smart about wearing masks, avoiding large groups and accepting the situation as best that I can. My daily mindfulness practices have been a great benefit in keeping me relatively calm this whole time.

I have also been called upon to be compassionate for many of the people who are and were suffering. The compassion took the form of wishing people to be happy and free from suffering and mourning the passing of two close friends who died of other causes during the pandemic. We'll explore compassion in detail in a later chapter.

To support our practice, we can think about the wisest response for any current situation. When we see things as they are, it is possible to find a place of peace right inside of us and respond to what is with appropriate and compassionate action.

The Japanese Zen poet Ikkyu writes,

> *What is the heart?*
> *But the voice*
> *Of the pine breeze,*
> *In a forgotten painting.*

HOW TO PRACTICE MINDFULNESS

When we practice mindfulness meditation, there are a couple of things that are relevant. First of all, in many traditions, you may have seen these yogis sitting cross legged on the floor or on a mat. They look like they are sitting totally upright and rigid, but after many years of experience, they are actually relaxed. When I was younger, I could practice this way.

I can remember a time when I was meditating in 1973 inside my van sitting in this yogic posture on my zafu (round cushion). I went into a deep meditation using my mantra that Swami Rama of the Himalayas had given me a couple of years earlier. This meditation became a turning point in my life and motivated me to learn to become a mindfulness meditation teacher.

The yogic position is just one of many postures you can use for mindfulness meditation. For example, I have found for the past four years that it is better for me to meditate lying down for my morning meditation and sometimes in the afternoon when I need a break, I'll meditate lying down on the couch. I often meditate in a sitting posture in my living room easy chair when I teach or participate in online classes. However, if you want to sit or lie down, it is okay with me. You will find other teachers and other situations where there is a prescribed way to sit.

Then there are certain positions of the hands and arms that some people are concerned about. These are called mudras and probably the most famous one is of the Buddha touching the earth as his witness to his enlightenment.

My position is that you don't need special mudras or special clothing or anything special to just sit down or lie down or stand or walk and meditate.

Then there is a choice of eyes closed or leaving them half way down. People can do what feels right for them.

Then we come to the objects of meditation. The most common object of meditation is the breath – the in breath and the out breath. When you breathe in, you know you are breathing in. When you breathe out, you know you are breathing out. This will be the meditation practice for this first chapter.

The other objects of meditation include sound – listening to my voice or anybody's voice or listening to the sounds in your room or your house as you practice meditation or the cars passing outdoors.

Then there are the sensations in the body. You feel your feet on the floor or wherever they are and how your hands lie gently on your lap peacefully, and they make contact with your thighs, perhaps. Whatever your position is, you can feel. Maybe you feel your sit bones, your buttocks, or your back against the chair. Even if you are standing or walking or lying down, you are in a suitable position to feel your sensations and they are suitable postures for doing meditation practice.

There are four aspects of practice that are really important. First of all, mindfulness is seeing things **just as they are** without judgment. This means seeing things in our lives without trying to change anything. This was manifested in the story about the Taoist farmer who accepted the horse leaving with the same attitude as the horse coming back with ten other horses.

The second one is learning to be present for whatever is happening right now, which I've mentioned before. For example, I have taken this practice of being mindful in everything I do – my emails, my web site, my family, my friends, folding the laundry, doing the dishes and putting away the laundry. I try to be present for all those activities. I encourage you to experiment with that. You can learn to be this way too by continuing to practice every day and then bringing mindfulness into daily life. Then, when you wash the dishes, you will only wash the dishes. You won't wash your problems, your worries, your plans or your anxieties. When you fold the laundry, you just fold the laundry. You don't fold your problems with the laundry. Remember, mindfulness is just a breath away!

The third aspect is to notice how things change. One of the main insights you get when you practice for some time is that nothing stays the same. This is called the law of impermanence and I'm sure you recognize this one way or another. Impermanence was one of the main factors that were taught by the Buddha. For example, we can't wait for bad things to end and we don't want good things to change. And both happen.

The fourth aspect is something I've written about before: not to judge our experience. Remember the story of the Taoist farmer.

You may want to put your book down right now and take a breath and notice how your body is connected to the earth. Are your feet on the floor? What about your thighs and hips? Are they touching the chair, couch or bed you are sitting or lying on? Just breathe! How does that feel?

YOUR FIRST MINDFULNESS MEDITATION PRACTICE

The first meditation practice the Buddha ever taught was

Mindfulness of Breathing. What is mindfulness of breathing?

It is actually quite simple but not easy. To be mindful of breathing you have to know when you are breathing in. You have to know when you are breathing out. You have to recognize a long breath as a long breath and you have to recognize a short breath as a short breath.

To practice mindfulness of breathing, find a comfortable position where you will not be disturbed for nine short minutes. This could be a cushion on the floor where you would sit with your back straight. You could also do the practice sitting in a comfortable chair or lying down in your bed or on the floor.

After a few weeks of practice of this nine-minute meditation, you can gradually begin to increase the length to twenty, thirty, or forty-five minutes, or whatever length is comfortable for you.

I chose nine minutes because it is fairly short and you should be able to find nine minutes sometime during your busy day. If you wish, you can set a timer on your cell phone or other device. I use the "Insight Timer" app on my iPhone which you can download for free from the App Store. Although this is preferred at the beginning, you can do without it, especially if you are taking your nine-minute meditation break on a bus, ferry, or train on your way to work or in your workplace.

If you would prefer to be guided in this practice, please visit the "First Mindfulness Meditation Practice" on the **Meditation Practices** website, mountainsangha.org, right under the "Mindfulness" menu item. There are five other guided meditations there, as well. You can listen to them on your smartphone or tablet using your web browser. Ear phones are recommended.

I recommend that you follow these instructions without judging them or thinking about them very much. Your experience will be unique to you and you should just follow them and take whatever you get. The most important advice I can give is to accept whatever happens, just as it is. Please don't hesitate to contact me if you have any questions. You'll find my contact information in the chapter, "About the Author."

The format of the instructions for practice consists of statements, comments, and ellipses. Statements are in shaded normal text as in this sentence. Each statement should be thought of as something that I say directly to you in a calming voice as if we were in the same room together. The comments are in brackets ([]), which provide additional information to supplement the instruction. The ellipses (...) indicate a pause for the period of an in breath and an out breath or slightly more. Repeated ellipses (... ... ...) indicate a break of one to five minutes or whatever you feel.

These instructions are virtually identical to instructions I give to my students in online classes as well as private clients. When I train people I follow along with them. The words below are typical of what I say in public or private sessions.

I recommend you first read each step of the instructions all the way through, then read one statement at a time, and then you can proceed at your own pace. Do not worry if you don't think you are doing it right – there is really no right or wrong way to do it. With practice, your mindfulness will become a lot easier. Eventually, you'll find your own way of practicing. Do not worry if you lose the sense or meaning of the current instruction because of thoughts, feelings, plans, memories, images, sounds, or emotions. Remember that these are just interruptions in meditation and are impermanent. Do not beat yourself up for them!

The Buddha taught that his teachings were like a raft taking us to the other shore. Once we get there, there is no reason to carry the raft further. We make our own path by walking it.

THE PRACTICE OF MINDFULNESS OF BREATHING

Step 1:
We begin by taking six deep breaths. When you breathe in..., breathe in completely and deeply..., filling your chest and abdomen as fully as possible... When you breathe out..., simply let go of all the air and the tensions you are holding... [Repeat a minimum of three to six times.]

Breathe in completely and deeply... Hold your breath for a count of three... Let go and release all the air in your lungs...

Breathe in deeply again... Hold for a count of three... Let go...

Breathe in again to your full capacity... Hold for a count of three... Breathe out and release...
In... in... in... One... Two... Three... Out... out... out...
Breathe in deeply again... Hold for a count of three... Let go...
Breathe in again to your full capacity... Hold for a count of three... Breathe out and release...
Now discontinue breathing deeply... and allow your breath to naturally return to normal... Take your time... Take it easy...

Step 2:
Now that your breathing has become normal... Withdraw yourself... into yourself... Become aware of your body... Notice how your body is connected to the earth... Open your senses... Taste inside your mouth and on your lips... The smell of air coming in your nostrils... Notice the ambient sounds... Don't become attached to them... Let them go... And sight... Eyes resting... insight opening... investigation opening... imagination opening... And touch... Notice your feet and legs... Notice your hips and pelvis... Notice your abdomen and lower back... Notice your rib cage and middle back... Notice your chest and upper back... Be aware of your shoulders... On down to your arms, hands and fingers... Notice your neck and the back of your head... Notice your face...
Continue to breathe naturally...
[Now continue being aware of your body until you are ready to move on.]
Be aware... of no other spaces... but these spaces...
Be aware... of no other times... but these times...
Be here... Be now... Be here, now...

Step 3:
Now settle back into your breathing...
When you breathe in..., know that you are breathing in...
When you breathe out..., know that you are breathing out...
When you breathe in..., you might say to yourself..., "Breathing in, I know I am breathing in"...
When you breathe out..., you might say to yourself...,

"Breathing out, I know I am breathing out"...
   Try this several times...
   "Breathing in, I know I'm breathing in... Breathing out, I know I'm breathing out..."
   If a thought comes into your mind..., just acknowledge it and return to your breath...
   You can shorten these, if you want...
   When you breathe in..., say to yourself, "In"...
   When you breathe out..., say to yourself, "Out"...
   Continue to pay attention to your breathing...
   "In... [in breath] Out..." [out breath]
   If a feeling comes into your body..., just allow it to be there..., and return to awareness of breathing...
   "In... Out..."
   If a sensation grabs your attention..., feel it..., recognize it..., accept it..., and return to your breathing...
   "In... Out..."
   If that errand you need to run... keeps cycling through your mind... let it be there for a while..., and then in your own time..., return to your breathing...
   "In... "Out..."
   If you notice a disturbing feeling... coming into your awareness..., acknowledge it..., and return to your breathing....
   [Continue this practice for at least five minutes, letting go of thoughts, feelings, etc., as above. You will most likely begin to notice that your in breath becomes deeper and your out breath becomes slower. Remember to handle interruptions and distractions by noticing them and letting them go. Notice what comes up for you. Allow it to be there for a while. Then return to your awareness of breathing.]
   [When the bell on your timer rings, or you learn that your nine-minute meditation period is over, slowly open your eyes and return to your normal daily activities. It may be a good idea to write down any thoughts or insights that you have experienced during your meditation session. Keeping a journal of this sort can be very beneficial.]

Step 4:
Now it is time to begin to return to the room... Once again..., bring your attention to your body... And in your own time..., come back to the room... Open your eyes...and say to yourself: May the merits of our practice benefit all beings and bring peace!

You may feel your breath mostly in your abdomen, chest, throat, windpipe, or nostrils. You can choose whichever place you want to focus on, as long as it feels natural to you.

Instead of using "In," when you breathe in, and "Out," when you breathe out, you can actually choose your own set of word triggers, based on your experience. For example, ever since I have had cancer, I have used "Healthy" on the in-breath and "Free" on the outbreath. If you experience your breath deeply in your abdomen, you can use a very old technique of repeating "Rising" when you breathe in and "Falling" when you breathe out.

In Zen practice, they teach counting the inhalations or the exhalations from one to ten, repeatedly. If you use this technique and lose the count, simply begin again.

Speaking of losing the count, there undoubtedly will be times when your mind is flooded with "shoulds" and "have tos" and you are distracted from your breathing. When this happens, simply bring your mind back to your breathing and place whatever crossed your mind into the back of your mind to be attended to later. Let these kinds of thoughts go as if they were white clouds drifting across the clear blue sky or the sound of a bird flying past your window.

Distractions happen frequently, even for the most experienced meditators. They have learned to let them go and return to their object of meditation, in this case, their breathing in and out, without further ado. Don't let it worry you or give you the feeling of failure if your session is full of thoughts and distractions. Consider them part of your learning process. Sharon Salzberg, one of the seminal teachers of insight meditation wrote,

> "What we are actually practicing is the art of beginning again, not accumulating a tally of more & more breaths

before our attention wanders. As we hone the ability to let go of distraction, to begin again without rancor or judgment, we are deepening forgiveness & compassion for ourselves. And in life, we find we might make a mistake, and more easily begin again, or stray from our chosen course & begin again. We are practicing this in meditation whether we are working with the breath, or awareness of body or emotions, or doing the formal phrases of loving kindness practice."

Please remember that it is more important to meditate than to worry about improving your meditation skills. Consistency is more important than technique when you are first beginning to meditate.

For more details, and for guided meditation practices of this type of meditation, please visit the **Meditation Practices** website, mountainsangha.org and visit each of the mindfulness meditation practices under the menu, *"Mindfulness,"* just below the banner.

For a detailed online meditation course, try **9 Minute Meditation**, 2wellbeing.org, where you will learn more than a dozen different meditation practices to try out at your own pace. Not all of the information is available when you sign up. Lessons are made available at the rate of three or four a week.

CHILDREN'S PRACTICE – PEBBLE MEDITATION

The following children's practice is good for children from three to 103. It is a simple practice created by Zen Master Thich Nhat Hanh specifically for children attending retreats at one of the Plum Village monasteries.

At some of the retreats, the children are given a small pouch in which to hold four pebbles of their own choosing. At other retreats, children are invited to bring their own pouches and pebbles. Sometimes, all that is needed are four pebbles. I have taught this practice to my three year old granddaughter, Ada.

The children are invited to sit in a quiet place and to arrive with an attitude of calmness. They sit down in a circle together. They can also do this in the quiet of their own homes with a brother or sister, a mom or dad, or by themselves.

To practice pebble meditation, please find a quiet place or go to your room if you are home and follow these steps.

Step 1:

Begin by settling into your seat and taking three deep breaths to calm your mind and open your heart... Place the four pebbles on the ground on your left... Pick up the first pebble with your left hand and place it in your right hand. This first pebble represents a flower. A flower is fresh. You are fresh... Now take two minutes to breathe in and breathe out with the pebble in your right hand... When you breathe in, you might say to yourself, "Breathing in, I see myself as a flower..." When you breathe out, you might say to yourself, "Breathing out, I feel fresh..." With some experience, you might be able to say to yourself, "Flower," when you breathe in and "Fresh" when you breathe out... After about two minutes, place the pebble on the ground on your right side...

Step 2:

Pick up the second pebble with your left hand and place it in your right hand... This second pebble represents a mountain... A mountain is solid... You are solid... You have the solid support of your parents, your family, your teachers, your friends... Now take two minutes to breathe in and breathe out with the pebble in our right hand... When you breathe in, you might say to yourself, "Breathing in, I see myself as a mountain..." When you breathe out, you might say to yourself, "Breathing out, I feel solid..." With some experience, you might be able to say to yourself, "Mountain," when you breathe in and "Solid" when you breathe out... After about two minutes, place the pebble on the ground on your right side...

Step 3:

Pick up the third pebble with your left hand and place it in your right hand... This third pebble represents still, clear water... Still water reflects what is clear, what is true... You are like the still water, reflecting what is true... You have the clarity of a young person... Now take two minutes to breathe in and breathe out with the pebble in our right hand... When you breathe in, you might say to yourself, "Breathing in, I see myself as still, clear water..." When you breathe out, you might say to yourself, "Breathing out, I reflect things as they are..." With some experience, you might be able to say to yourself, "Water," when you breathe in and "Reflecting" when you breathe out... After about two minutes, place the pebble on the ground on your right side...

Step 4:
Pick up the last pebble with your left hand and place it in your right hand... This fourth pebble represents space... Space represents freedom... You are like space and you are free... Now take two minutes to breathe in and breathe out with the pebble in our right hand... When you breathe in, you might say to yourself, "Breathing in, I see myself as space..." When you breathe out, you might say to yourself, "Breathing out, I feel free..." With some experience, you might be able to say to yourself, "Space," when you breathe in and "Free" when you breathe out... After about two minutes, place the pebble on the ground on your right side...

Step 5:
When you are finished, take a few moments to think about your experience of the four steps... When you are ready, pick up the four pebbles with your right hand and place them in your pouch...

After you complete the pebble meditation several times, you will become sensitive to the four qualities that the meditation inspires: freshness, solidity, calmness and spaciousness. Then, when you feel angry or irritated or sad, you can think of the flower and begin to return to the feeling of freshness of the flower inside yourself. When you feel frightened or uneasy, you can think of the mountain and begin to feel solid in yourself. When things get a little confusing or unclear or bad emotions come up, you can think of the clear lake which reflects what is real, what is true and then you know you can become calm also. And if you feel trapped or bored or just don't know what to do or you can't do what you want to do, you can think of spaciousness and begin to feel a little freedom. Then all the anger, fear and sadness can be transformed into happiness, joy and freedom.

If you have a pouch, you can bring it everywhere you go and know that freedom is possible. This way, you will always have your freshness, solidity, calmness and spaciousness with you as well.

In Plum Village, there is a song that goes with the pebble meditation or as a stand-alone song. There are many renditions of this song on YouTube. The words of the song are:

> *Breathing in, breathing out*
> *Breathing in, breathing out*
> *I am blooming as a flower*
> *I am fresh as the dew.*
> *I am solid as a mountain*
> *I am firm as the earth*
> *I am free*
> *Breathing in, breathing out*
> *Breathing in, breathing out*
> *I am water reflecting,*
> *What is real, what is true*
> *And I feel there is space*
> *Deep inside of me*
> *I am free*
> *I am free*
> *I am free*

CHAPTER 2: WORKING WITH EMOTIONS

If you did even one minute of practice with mindfulness of breathing or the children's practice, you may have noticed that thoughts arose. You may have noticed that some feelings also arose. These thoughts and feelings come unbidden and much of the time, they don't mean anything. For me, sometimes I get lost in the thoughts so much that I forget I am supposed to be meditating. Sometimes I feel pain or discomfort. Sometimes my feelings get carried away and I am gone – no longer meditating.

It's pretty easy to get lost in thought while you are meditating. Ajahn Buddhadasa, a famous and influential Thai Buddhist master of the last century, once said, "Lost in thought," when referring to the influence of Western materialism. You see, people go walking around without noticing their environment and are completely lost in thought – about their work, their families, their community, whatever. They don't notice other people. They don't notice the faces of other people. They fail to see the sparkling eyes of the baby passing them in the stroller. They don't notice the beautiful flowers, trees and other wonders of life. They look down at the concrete with their phones to their ears.

Many years ago, I noticed that I was getting lost in thought when I would go on walks and I found it to be very unpleasant. To remedy this, I turned my walking for exercise into walking meditation. When I lift my left foot, I make a mental note of "healthy." When I lift my right foot, I make a mental note of "free." All the while, I am looking around the environment for flowers, birds, trees, mountains, rivers, creeks and people. When I pass someone, I invariably say "Hello," or wave to them. Most of the time, people respond and I am OK when they don't. Sometimes, I say to them under my voice, "May you be free." This is an example of loving kindness in daily life.

Thich Nhat Hanh said,

> *Walking meditation is really to enjoy the walking - walking not in order to arrive, just for walking, to be in the present moment, and to enjoy each step.*

You can learn to walk like this. If it is helpful, you might use the word "lifting" when you lift your right foot and "placing" when you place your right foot. The same words can be used with your left foot.

So how do we deal with thoughts, feelings and emotions as they arise in our meditation practice? First of all, we should notice that thoughts and feelings and emotions are a normal part of being totally human. There is nothing wrong with having thoughts, feelings and emotions and we want to be able to work skillfully with them. We also have to cope with the highs and lows of life and in this chapter, we will address some of these issues.

You may have noticed that before any recognition of a thought, feeling or emotion takes place, there is some kind of sensation in the body. And this sensation is pleasant, unpleasant or neutral. You have an inkling that this is good or this is terrible. Or you may not know if it's good or bad, if it's nice or rotten or whatever. It can be pleasant, unpleasant or neutral. On top of that, we have the idea of what this sensation is all about. This is called the perception of the sensation – our interpretation. It could be anger, love, resentment, understanding. All emotions come and go.

We get tossed around by what we call the "Worldly Winds." We all want praise and no blame. We all want gain and no loss. We all want pleasure and no pain. We all want fame and no disrepute. The worldly winds can distort our judgment, distract us from being present and cause our mind to go into "*If Only...*" mind.

I would be happy *if only* I could win the lottery and become a millionaire. I would be happy *if only* I could find the right man or woman to spend my life with. I could be happy if only I had the right car or house or whatever. "*If only*" mind really doesn't help. I know this from personal experience. "If only I had the perfect girlfriend," was a common experience for me in my 20s.

We know these emotions come up. We get mad. We get happy. We get glad to be with people we love. We sometimes get bored. There is a whole scale of these emotions. Our job, if we choose to accept it, is to recognize these emotions and not allow them to rule our lives. We need to nourish them and wash them away so they don't affect us on any deep level, unless we want them to.

What helps most when thoughts or emotions arise during meditation is not to identify with them. They are just like the sound of a passing car or the sound of a bird outside your window. They are like waves on the ocean not realizing that they are all water. They are like the blink of an eye or cycle of breath. They come and they go. Our job is not to recognize that they are impermanent and will not last long. This will teach us to respond to the thoughts or emotions rather than reacting to them.

We may also notice that some thoughts and emotions come with the idea that they are pleasant. And guess what, we want to have more of them – we get greedy. We may notice that some of them are unpleasant and we want them to cease, and we get lost in thought over them. S. N. Goenka, an Indian teacher of Vipassana meditation who was born in Myanmar, put it this way (emphasis mine):

> *Arising and Passing*
> *Whether pleasant, unpleasant, or neutral, gross or subtle, every sensation shares the same characteristic: it arises and passes away, arises and passes away. It is this arising and passing that we have to experience through practice, not just accept as truth because Buddha said so, not just accept because intellectually it seems logical enough to us. We must experience sensation's nature, understand its flux, and **learn not to react to it**.*

There are certain techniques that we can use when we recognize that we are in a bad way with an emotion. For example, the day I taught the class on emotions, my daughter was visiting from Spain. We had a nice drive out to the cliffs above Bodega Bay and had a wonderful hike. When we came back, I was confronted with lots of computer problems, and that was not too good. I really felt frustrated. So I bit the bullet, restarted the computer and things started to work out. I recognized that I was in that excited state of being unregulated and stressed out. I was able to bring myself out of it by allowing it to be there and then deciding on an action I could take that would alleviate those dreadful emotions.

What I did was to invoke the RAIN acronym:
- **R**ecognize what is going on
- **A**llow the experience to be there, just as it is
- **I**nvestigate with interest and care
- **N**ourish with self-compassion

I **recognized** that I was under stress from the problems I was having with the computer. I acknowledged my thoughts, feelings and behaviors that were affecting me and knew that I was in some state of dysregulation. I felt stuck and unable to drop my constricting sensation, beliefs and emotions.

Then, I simply began to **allow** all the thoughts, feelings and emotions to be there without trying to fix anything or avoid anything. I didn't agree with my situation and I allowed it to be just as it is. I don't quite remember how I managed to silence the painful feelings, and they managed to quiet down after some time.

Next, I **investigated** why I was having such a problem with the computer and remembered that this has happened many times in my career of software engineering. They were par for the course and only last as long as it takes you to fix the problem. The idea of regular occurrence of these problems put me a bit at ease. This curiosity about how often these problems occur enabled me to get through my feelings about the incident without judgment.

When you are in a similar situation, you could ask yourself some or all of the following questions: "What most wants attention? How am I experiencing this in my body? What am I believing? What does this vulnerable place want from me? What does it most need?"

Finally, I **nourished** myself with self-compassion, which is covered in detail in Chapter 7. I took some deep breaths and noticed my feet on the ground. I may have whispered to myself one or more of these phrases: *"I'm here with you. I'm sorry, and I love you. I love you, and I'm listening. It's not your fault. Trust in your goodness."* There is more about RAIN later in this chapter.

This brings me to the teaching on the *Window of Tolerance*, introduced by Dr. Dan Siegel. When we are in the window of tolerance, we feel like we can deal with life as it is evolving on a moment-by-moment or day-by-day basis. We are able to handle pressure or stress without much difficulty. When we are not in our window of tolerance, we are more likely to agitated and dysregulated and we are most likely in a state of "fight, flight or freeze." David Treleaven, author of *Trauma Sensitive Mindfulness*, said,

> ... when we're in our window, we're most likely to be stable, present, and regulated. When we are out of our window, we're more likely to be agitated, triggered, out of control or feeling dysregulated.

For example, I get triggered out of my window of tolerance when I have to wait on the phone for customer service and I'm talking to a robot. Not a person and I can't get that robot to connect me with a human being. It is especially bad with Comcast, which has an extremely difficult voice activation system to navigate. I get really turned off by that kind of stuff and, under certain circumstances, it is a necessary evil.

So it is really important for us to recognize when we get out of our window of tolerance and do something to come back to regulation. And one of the best things we can do to come back to regulation is to simply notice your feet touching the ground or your legs on the chair or your hands on your thighs if you are sitting. Feeling your feet on the ground is also helpful, if you are standing. Feeling you back supporting you if you are lying down could also work. You can also place one hand on your heart and another on your belly. Or you can cup your cheeks in your two hands. I've tried them all.

Our ability to return to regulation is called *resilience*. The greater our resilience, the faster we return to regulation. Continual practice in returning to regulation helps us with resilience and the more resilience we have the faster we can deal with whatever is happening in the here and now, in the present moment.

The following quote is from S. N. Goenka, a Burmese teacher

living in India. He is considered one of the founders of the modern insight meditation movement in the West. He taught a special kind of meditation known as Vipassana. My wife and daughter both took his ten day course in Bodh Gaya, India, perhaps 30 years apart. He was also a teacher for Jack Kornfield, Joseph Goldstein and Sharon Salzberg, the founders of the Insight Meditation Society in Barre, Massachusetts.

> *Whether pleasant, unpleasant, or neutral, gross or subtle, every sensation shares the same characteristic: it arises and passes away, arises and passes away. It is this arising and passing that we have to experience through practice, not just accept as truth because Buddha said so, not just accept because intellectually it seems logical enough to us. We must experience sensation's nature, understand its flux, and learn not to react to it. - S. N. Goenka, "Finding Sense in Sensation"*

This is one of the essential teachings that I have found about these pleasant and unpleasant feelings that they arise and pass away. There is a practice you can do to alleviate some arisen stress besides the grounding practice, above, and we call this the two question practice. This is a really good contemplation if you want to take some time to do it some later date. The first question is "What are my joys and how do I increase them?" The second question is "What are my sorrows and how do I decrease them?" You contemplate your joys and sorrows in this way and you want to embrace the joys. You want to recognize and allow and nurture the sad parts. These sad parts are unwholesome and cause suffering when you are feeling stressed out and you are feeling dysregulated and out of your window of tolerance. It's really important to have a mechanism of returning back to regulation. And I think this is a really good one.

You might also ask yourself, "What do you need to be happy and why are you not happy now?" These two questions also come into play and you can use them to investigate what's going on when a negative emotion arises in you and you find yourself caught into them.

Then there's this whole syndrome which took place in my 20s and 30s. Not so much in my 40s. In my 20s and 30s I had this habit of saying, "I'll be happy when..." This is another version of "If only" mind." As I said before, I am thankful that I grew out of it. I think it is some kind of illusion. "Happiness is here and now!" It is not in the future. Happiness is in the present moment and only in the present moment. That's the end of it. It's a happy time for me. My daughter was here with me along with other class members when I delivered this class.

HOW TO DEAL WITH AFFLICTED EMOTIONS

Mind and Store Consciousness

In order to understand how to deal with afflictive emotions, we first need to look at a model of the mind derived from the teachings of the Buddha and later meditation masters in a set of sutras (texts, writings) called Abidharma. For our purpose, we can think of the mind as a circle with a line across the center. The upper part is called "mind consciousness," and the lower part is called "store consciousness." Mind consciousness corresponds to what psychologists call the conscious mind – what is on our mind right now. Mind consciousness arises out of some kind of feeling or perception. It can be visual, auditory, olfactory, tasty or sensory. It can also be a thought, image, memory, plan or some other mental activity.

Store consciousness is similar to what psychologists call the subconscious mind and it is different in many respects. Store consciousness is said to contain the seeds of all possible mental formation, traditionally, only 51. It contains approximately 21 wholesome seeds like faith, tranquility, equanimity, joy, compassion, loving kindness, happiness and mindfulness. It also contains many more unwholesome seeds like anger, greed, craving, ignorance, aggression and many others that you can probably name without much effort.

So, for example, when the seed of anger arises in the mind it becomes active in mind consciousness. We are ready to fight or flight. Suppose we don't want to feel the anger right now. What can we do about it?

The first thing we can do is to invite the seed of mindfulness to arise into mind consciousness to recognize the anger. Once it is recognized, we can employ the energy of mindfulness to acknowledge the anger and know that it is present in our mind consciousness. Then we would be able to embrace our anger. We can say, "Hello my little anger. I am here for you." We hold the anger like we would our newborn baby.

At this point, we can look deeply and investigate the anger as much as we want because we are no longer in fight or flight mode. We are no long dysregulated. We feel regulated enough to gain insights into the causes and conditions that led to our anger in the first place. We can encourage the anger to go back into the garden of our store consciousness.

The more we do this kind of practice with most of our unwholesome emotions, the smaller the seeds become and the less frequently the rise up to our mind consciousness. The watering of the seed of mindfulness makes this happen over and over again and we begin to have more wholesome mind states than unwholesome. This can bring a lot of happiness, gratitude and joy to our lives. I know this is true from my own experience. I used to be very insecure in my relationships with friends. I would expect a lot from them. When I saw this tendency to occur, I would recognize it was happening and call upon my mindfulness to arise to take care of my insecurity. I would follow the process over and over until the seed of insecurity became so weak that it hardly arises anymore. When it does, I know what to do.

Please don't take my word for any of this! You have to discover your own path to dealing with your afflictive emotions. You can try to use the process above and see if it works for you. If it does, then you can make it part of your mindfulness practice and learn to not be tossed around by your unwholesome emotions.

RAELI

Thich Nhat Hanh wrote about this process in his book, *The Heart of Buddha's Teaching*, Chapter 6. He wrote,

When we have a strong emotion, we know it can be dangerous to act, but we don't have the strength or clarity to refrain. We have to learn the art of breathing in and out, stopping our activities, and calming our emotions. We have to learn to become solid and stable like an oak tree, and not be blown from side to side by the storm. The Buddha taught many techniques to help us calm our body and mind and look deeply at them. They can be summarized in five stages:
(1) Recognition — If we are angry, we say, "I know that anger is in me."
(2) Acceptance — When we are angry, we do not deny it. We accept what is present.
(3) Embracing — We hold our anger in our two arms like a mother holding her crying baby. Our mindfulness embraces our emotion, and this alone can calm our anger and ourselves.
(4) Looking deeply — When we are calm enough, we can look deeply to understand what has brought this anger to be, what is causing our baby's discomfort.
(5) Insight — The fruit of looking deeply is understanding the many causes and conditions, primary and secondary, that have brought about our anger, that are causing our baby to cry. Perhaps our baby is hungry. Perhaps his diaper pin is piercing his skin. Our anger was triggered when our friend spoke to us meanly, and suddenly we remember that he was not at his best today because his father is dying. We reflect like this until we have some insights into what has caused our suffering. With insight, we know what to do and what not to do to change the situation.

To help with RAELI, we can ask ourselves questions like, "What do I need right now to be with this emotion?" Or "How can I take care of myself if I can't be with it?"

RAIN

A similar process to the one above was introduced by Michele McDonald. It has been modernized by Tara Brach, author and founder of Insight Meditation Center of Washington DC. She covered a lot of situations for which RAIN is useful in her book, *Radical Compassion: Learning to Love Yourself and Your World with the Practice of RAIN*. Her many talks and guided meditation are available on her website. Remember, she is one of the two main teachers for the Mindfulness Meditation Teacher Certification Training that was the inspiration for this book.

RAIN is an acronym that can be used as a tool to practice mindfulness and compassion. The four steps are:

R – Recognize what is going on. This is the same as the "R" in RAELI, above.

A – Allow the experience to be there, just as it is. This is the same as the "A" in RAELI.

I – Investigate the experience with interest and care. This is equivalent to the "L" (looking deeply) in RAELI

N – Nurture with self-compassion. This relates to the "E" in RAELI. When we embrace our suffering, self-compassion begins to arise once we realize we are suffering. This is the key, though – to recognize we are suffering. It comes to fruition when we intentionally embrace what is happening inside and around us and offer ourselves some self-care. We can comfort ourselves by mentally whispering phrases like, "I'm here with you." "I'm sorry, and I love you." "I love you, and I'm listening." "It's not your fault." "Trust in your goodness."

We may even feel like comforting ourselves by placing a hand on our heart or cheek or back of the neck. We can also imagine a person we know loves us unconditionally sending us love, wisdom and comfort to us. When we turn towards love with the intention to be self-compassionate, it will help us nurture our hearts.

Tara added a fifth step in the book called "After the rain." After the RAIN, we pause. We relax. We open to our experiences and we allow it all to be there. We become calm and at ease.

I have also taught a similar experience called RAINS for exploring and savoring wonder experiences which we will get to in a later chapter. The "S" stands for savoring the experience you come up with. Please stay tuned.

WORKING WITH THOUGHTS

Like emotions and feelings, thoughts can creep into our mindfulness practice and disturb our concentration. These can be in the form of plans and to-do lists, memories, images, problem solving, judging, worrying, fearing, interesting thought, creative thought, painful thought and others. The point is not to get lost in the story of the thought. The Zen poet Gensel writes,

> "Trailing my stick, I go down to the garden edge and call to a monk to go out with me to the pine gate... The spring floods have washed away the planks of the bridge. Shouldering our sandals, we wade the narrow stream... I dabble in the flow delighted by the shallowness of the stream now, gaze at the flagging, admiring how firm the stones are. The point in life is to know what's enough. Why envy those otherworld immortals? With the happiness held in one inch-square heart, you can fill the whole space between heaven and earth."

When we are in a place like that, who needs thoughts? And what good would they do? Yet we know that it is easy to get "lost in thought," as Ajan Buddhasa, a Thai forest monk said when how the modern world appeared to him.

Thoughts seem to be really constant. When we realize that our thoughts and beliefs run our lives, we wonder how we can stop them. The truth is, we can't! They will come as certain as summer follows spring or as night follows day. We live in a world of thought.

And we have to remember that most of our modern world was first a thought in someone's brain. They used their creativity to mine the coal which drives our factories to produce just about everything we depend on for life. Someone thought of a "horseless carriage," and now we have automobiles, trucks, trains, airplanes and ships larger than many cities. These modern sensational conveniences all began with a thought that was developed into a plan. The plan was drawn out on paper and calculations were made. Then the things were manufactured and distributed all over the world. "Long live thought!"

Yet, as the Buddha once asked, "Who is our enemy?" and he answered,

> *"Mind is your enemy. No one can harm you more than a mind untrained. Who is your friend? Mind is your friend. No one can assist you and care for you better than your mind well-trained. Not even the most loving mother or father."*

Without knowing much about thoughts, beginning meditators worry a lot about the waterfall of thoughts when they meditate. They often give up because of this. These thoughts keep coming and they have not yet learned what to do. For others, the realization of the stream of thoughts motivates them to learn how to control them. Carlos Castaneda wrote,

> *"You talk to yourself too much. You're not unique in that--every one of us does. We maintain our world with our inner dialogue, and yet a man or woman of knowledge is aware that the world will change completely as soon as they stop talking to themselves."*

To see for yourself how thoughts plague you, try this 30 second test. Set a timer on your watch or phone for 30 seconds and count how many thoughts you have. When the bell rings, notice how high you have counted. Did you have 5-10 thoughts or more than 30?

It really doesn't matter how many thoughts you had because that is not an indicator of how well you will do when you meditate. The point is that the thoughts are there. We can't stop them. And we can learn not to follow the story of our thoughts. Remember what Mark Twain said? "I've had a lot of worries in my life, most of which never happened." Or "I am an old man, and I have known a great many troubles, but most of them never happened." In addition, many of our thoughts are repeated over and over again. I've heard from Jack Kornfield that 90% of our thoughts are repeated!

When we practice, we begin to notice the thought process itself. Are we thinking about the past most of the time? Are we in the future? Are they worried about money, jobs, security or health or judging someone or something? Remember the story about the Taoist farmer? Just notice the quality of your thoughts from time to time. After a while, we will begin to look with kindness and loving awareness at our thoughts and they won't have so much control over us. Thich Nhat Hanh asks us, "Is it so?" when referring to our thoughts.

The technique we use is to first, just name the thought. Are we planning? Note, "planning." Are we remembering? Note "remembering." Or judging, doubting, imagining or whatever. Just make note of the thought and allow it to dissipate like the sound of a passing car or the sound of a bird outside our window, as happened this morning. Thoughts rise and fall like waves of the ocean or the breath going in and out.

Remember, thoughts are normal and human. Everyone has thoughts. We have planning thoughts, judging thoughts, anxious thoughts, loving thoughts and many other kinds of thoughts. Remember to simply hold them lightly and they will dissipate like a cloud in the sky. Ghaung Tzu, like Lao Tzu (author of the famous Tao Te Ching) was a Taoist sage. He wrote,

> "If a man is crossing a river--" or a woman crossing a river-- "and an empty boat collides with their skiff, even though they'd be a bad-tempered person, they will not be shouting and not be angry. But if there's a man in the other boat, they will shout at them to steer clear and shout again angrily, and all because there is someone in the boat. Yet if you can empty your own boat crossing the river of the world, no one will oppose you and no one will seek to harm you."

So you see, our thoughts can get in the way of how we interpret events in our lives. Sometimes, you may be walking in the woods and you think you see a snake on the ground and you get afraid. Will this snake bite me and cause me to be ill or die? Then you notice it is just a piece of old rope and you walk on without fear.

Our technique is to name our thoughts, normalize them and make light of them. We learn not to believe in them very much. We do this instead of hanging on to our beliefs. First, we notice the content of our thoughts by counting planning thoughts, worried thoughts, judging thoughts, creative thoughts, etc. Once we master the content of our thoughts, we can begin to name them so they dissolve like salt in water. Then we notice how insubstantial they are like a flash of lightning or a passing bird. We begin to realize that our thoughts aren't real. They come for a while, last for a little and pass away – we notice that they are impermanent.

With awareness, it is possible for us to play a little with our thoughts without struggling against them. To illustrate this, the Dalai Lama says, "Some of your thoughts do not have your best interest in mind. So why would you continue to think about them?" When we remember that we are not our thoughts, we can begin to cultivate thoughts of loving kindness, compassion, sympathetic joy, equanimity, gratitude, generosity (see later chapters) and other wholesome thoughts that can benefit many other people. We awaken out of the dream of forgetfulness and develop an attitude of interest, humor and lightness towards our thoughts, as the poet Kaveri Patel writes,

> "There's a monkey in my mind swinging on a trapeze reaching back to the past or leaning into the future, never standing still. Sometimes I want to kill that monkey, shoot it square between the eyes so I won't have to think anymore or feel the pain of worry. But today, I thanked her, and she jumped down straight into my lap, trapeze still swinging as we sat still."

THE PRACTICE OF MINDFULNESS OF THOUGHTS AND EMOTIONS

The practice of mindfulness of thoughts and emotions follows along with the practice of mindfulness of breathing. We begin just like the first meditation with six deep breaths, and settling into our bodies. We continue to practice mindfulness of breathing with the intention of noticing our thoughts, naming them, and letting them dissolve like salt in water, like the sound of a passing bird, like the melting of ice in the beginning of spring.

In this meditation, I will invite you to choose an anchor onto which to settle your mind during the meditation. Most commonly, this will be the breath, which works for most people. Other anchors are also possible such as your feet on the ground, the sounds in your room, outside or passing by or a mantra, your hands on your hips, your buttocks on the chair or sofa, a taste in your mouth or an odor in your room. Your eyes may be closed or open slightly, so you could focus on a mental image.

Ready? Choose your anchor and let's begin. Steps 1 and 2 are the same as in mindfulness of breathing.

Step 1:
We begin by taking six deep breaths. When you breathe in..., breathe in completely and deeply..., filling your chest and abdomen as fully as possible... When you breathe out..., simply let go of all the air and the tensions you are holding... [Repeat a minimum of three to six times.]
Breathe in completely and deeply... Hold your breath for a count of three... Let go and release all the air in your lungs...
Breathe in deeply again... Hold for a count of three... Let go...
Breathe in again to your full capacity... Hold for a count of three... Breathe out and release...
In... in... in... One... Two... Three... Out... out... out...
Breathe in deeply again... Hold for a count of three... Let go...
Breathe in again to your full capacity... Hold for a count of three... Breathe out and release...
Now discontinue breathing deeply... and allow your breath to naturally return to normal... Take your time... Take it easy...

Step 2:
Now that your breathing has become normal... Withdraw yourself... into yourself... Become aware of your body... Notice how your body is connected to the earth... Open your senses... Taste

inside your mouth and on your lips... The smell of air coming in your nostrils... Notice the ambient sounds... Don't become attached to them... Let them go... And sight... Eyes resting... insight opening... investigation opening... imagination opening... And touch... Notice your feet and legs... Notice your hips and pelvis... Notice your abdomen and lower back... Notice your rib cage and middle back... Notice your chest and upper back... Be aware of your shoulders... On down to your arms, hands and fingers... Notice your neck and the back of your head... Notice your face...
Continue to breathe naturally...
[Now continue being aware of your body until you are ready to move on.]
Be aware... of no other spaces... but these spaces...
Be aware... of no other times... but these times...
Be here... Be now... Be here, now...

Step 3:
I invite you to bring your attention to your body... Note there is a body... If you are sitting on a chair and your feet are on the rug or carpet or floor, notice how your feet are in touch with the earth... If you are lying down on a bed or couch you can notice how your body is connected to the earth through the bed or couch... Just notice how you are connected to the earth... ...

Now I invite you to bring your attention to your breathing if that works for you... If it doesn't, please select another anchor for your mind... If it is comfortable for you, you might choose to whisper mentally to yourself "In" when you breathe in... You might say to yourself "Out" when you breathe out... Or simply note your in breath and your out breath...

As soon as you notice a strong sensation in your body, shift your attention to that sensation... Be with this sensation as best as you can... Notice its characteristics... Is it changing? ... Is it getting weaker? ... Can you be with it? ... If it is difficult to be with, please find another place in your body that you can be with... When the sensation dissipates, return to your breath or whatever anchor you have chosen...

If you notice a strong emotion arising, shift your attention to the feeling... Notice where you feel it in your body... Is it getting stronger? ... Notice how the feeling tone changes... What is happening now? ... Can you be with the feeling? ... If not, why not? ... After some time the feeling may no longer require attention so you can shift your attention back to your breathing or other anchor...

If you notice a compelling thought occupying your mind, shift your attention to the thought... Notice the thought... What are its chief characteristics? ... Can you name the thought? ... Is it a planning thought? ... Are you remembering something? ... Are you judging someone? ... Are you worrying about something? ... Are you imagining something? ... Is it a painful thought? ... Or a fearful thought? ... Or a happy thought? ... Is it quite repetitive? ... Or changing? ... Name it just as it is... Notice that it will dissolve like salt in water... Notice that the thought is ephemeral, empty and has no substance... Unless we make it so...

After the thought dissipates, return to your breathing or other anchor of meditation... If another sensation, emotion or thought arises, handle it once again with mindfulness... When it subsides, return to your anchor...

[Continue this practice for at least five minutes, letting go of thoughts, emotions and sensations as above. You will most likely begin to notice that your in breath becomes deeper and your out breath becomes slower. Remember to handle interruptions and distractions by noticing them and letting them go. Notice what comes up for you. Allow it to be there for a while. Then return to your awareness of breathing.]

[When the bell on your timer rings, or you learn that your nine-minute meditation period is over, slowly open your eyes and return to your normal daily activities. It may be a good idea to write down any thoughts or insights that you have experienced during your meditation session. Keeping a journal of this sort can be very beneficial.]

Thank you for your practice. How did it go for you? What did you notice that was wholesome? What did you notice that was difficult? How did you handle the difficulty?

CHILDREN'S PRACTICE

If you have been practicing pebble meditation with your children, then this would be a good time to introduce them to deep breathing exercises for coming back to their true home and being present in the here and the now. I have found that children really love this practice. You could practice with them when you put them to bed. You could say something like this:

"Sweetheart, are you feeling comfortable in your bed right now?" If they say, "Yes," then proceed with the practice below. If they say "No," then ask them, "What are you feeling right now?" Then listen deeply to their answer and repeat back to them how they are feeling. Ask them if they can be with that feeling just as it is. It is hard to do the bedtime practice if they are uncomfortable. They may need a hug or some soothing object like the little giraffe that my granddaughter, Ada cherishes so much. Comforting them is more important than the practice, so continue along these lines until they are comforted.

Proceed to invite them to take three deep and complete breaths with you doing so beside them. Remember their lungs are quite small compared to yours so don't make them try to keep up with your deep breaths. You might ask them to feel their heads on the pillow or their back on the mattress or their toes touching the top sheet or their connection anywhere with their body. You might ask them, "Where do you feel your body on the bed the strongest?"

Now say to them, "Withdraw yourself into yourself and become aware of your body. Can you feel your body? Where do you feel your body the most?" Listen deeply to their answer and say to them, "May your body be safe and secure, strong and healthy, accepted and loved." Pause frequently so they can take in the feeling of their body being safe and secure.

Next, say to them, "Be aware of no other spaces but these spaces [the spaces in their body, bed and room, if explanation is required]. Be aware of no other times but this time. Be here. Be now. Be here now." Pause for a minute or so to allow them to arrive in the here and now.

Now ask them, "What happened today that you are grateful

for?" It could be a visit to grandpa and grandma or the afternoon in the playground or spending time with a friend. Take whatever they say without judgment and ask them to think about that happy time while they drift off to sleep.

CHAPTER 3: UNDERSTANDING HAPPINESS

His Holiness the 14th Dalai Lama is famous for saying, "We all want to be happy and avoid suffering, and we all have a right to be happy. That's why I say we are all the same."

So what does it mean to be happy? How do we find happiness? Doesn't everyone want to be happy and not suffer? Will we find happiness in true love? Will we find happiness in great wealth? Will we find happiness with great power? What does it take for us to be truly happy?

I have already told the story of how my children have brought me great happiness and joy. They have taught me a lot about what it means to be a father. They have taught me a lot about being present for someone else. This was a very important thing for me to learn. It became for me the motivation to write this book so that more parents can be there for their children, so that more parents can be present enough to understand their children.

For example, you might recall that my daughter Jessica married an Italian and lives in Barcelona. From an early age, she learned not to accumulate things and to accumulate experience. She must have known about this instinctively because immediately after completing a double major in journalism and Spanish at the University of Oregon, she went off to Jaen, Spain, right in the olive growing region, to teach English to Spanish children. The next year, she did the same in Cadiz. Then she was home for a few months and then went to live in the Amazon Rain Forest with the Achuar natives to help them with their English. After four months, she moved to Quito and worked for a travel company. The next fall, she moved to the Galapagos to teach English once again and after four months, moved back to Quito. She made lifelong friends wherever she went. Then she got the idea to get a Master's degree from the University of Barcelona and moved there in October, 2013, and has remained there ever since. She and her husband have put travel and being with friends more important than anything else in their lives. Fortunately, we have been able to visit her in Spain several times.

My experience was quite different from hers. I spent six years in graduate school studying physics with an "If only..." mind. "If only I get my degree." "If only I marry a beautiful woman." "If only I become a millionaire." "If only..." "If only..." "If only..." You get the picture. I was caught in "If only..." mind and confused about what would make me happy until I realized that it had to come from the inside.

I think a lot of people share my confusion and I think this is because we really don't understand what will make us happy in the long run. We have a remarkable number of misunderstandings and misconceptions about what it takes to be happy.

MISCONCEPTIONS ABOUT HAPPINESS

A lot of people have misconceptions about their happiness. They think that if they get a good job, they will be happy. And they are happy for some period of time and then they return back to their normal state. When they get a raise, once again they are happy for a month or two, but they again settle back to their normal state.

Scientific studies have shown that people's expectations about how unhappy they will be when they don't get a good job that they applied for are terribly misleading. For example, on a scale of 1 to 10 where 10 is total happiness and 1 is not happy at all, research has found that most people think their drop in happiness would be about two points, when in this research, the actual drop is a little more than one half a point. This result was for what they thought was a fair decision. When they thought it was an unfair decision, there was no drop in happiness.

Another misconception comes from misunderstanding what is a good job. Research has found that recent grads mostly want high compensation and a balance between work and life. So what counts as high compensation? The thing is whatever our compensation, we think it should be higher. Suppose you are making $100,000 per year. How much do you really need? The fallacy is that every time we get more money we think we need more.

But does money really make us happier? Research findings state that there is only a very weak correlation between money and happiness, unless you live in a poorer country. Once you get enough money for your basic needs, money has a negligible effect on life satisfaction. There is an old joke that goes something like this: "Money can't buy happiness but it can make you awfully comfortable while you are miserable!" Isn't this the fate of the ultra-rich who can't buy happiness with all their money? Their suffering is totally locked up in trying to get more, to be number one in the state, country or world. In actuality, researchers have found that high income doesn't equal happiness but it does bring you a life that you think is better.

When I was a college student many years ago, I was at home in St. Louis visiting my family. I was the oldest of six. My baby sister, Brenda, was perhaps four or five years old. My great uncle Harry, who was a very rich man, was over for dinner and commented on how cute my baby sister Brenda was. He said something like, "You wouldn't give her up for ..." I stepped in and said, "Your money." Everything went quiet. You see, Uncle Harry had helped my father establish his business and my dad probably owed him a lot of money at that time. I had no idea back then that my dad was so indebted to Uncle Harry.

I think it is important to point out that B. Alan Wallace, a prominent Buddhist scholar says,

> "One of the best-kept secrets is that the happiness we're striving for so desperately in the perfect spouse, the great kids, the fine job, security, excellent health, and good looks has always been within and is just waiting to be unveiled. Knowing that what we are seeking comes from within changes everything."

Let's consider this fantasy about a family of four. The father, Richard, has a clothing store that brings in enough money that his wife, Michelle, can be a stay-at-home mom and take care of the children. Their son, Chris, is 13 going on 18 and their daughter, Emma, is 11 and already showing signs of puberty. On the whole we can say that their average happiness rating on a scale of 1 to 10, where 10 is totally happy and 1 is, well, you know, not so great, is

7, let's say.

One day Richard decides to buy a lottery ticket just for fun. It turns out that he wins five million dollars. His happiness rating soars to 10 as does the rest of the family. They plan a summer trip to Lisbon, Barcelona, Rome, Paris, Berlin and London, expecting to be gone for about four weeks. They fly first class and stay in the best hotels. They love everything about their trip and they all are now at happiness level 10.

They come back to their home in Davenport, Iowa and the kids start school in a new district because they upgraded their house to the best neighborhood in Davenport, using the money from the lottery. The kids are busy making new friends. Chris is now 14 and Emma is 12, a budding beauty. After things settle down around Thanksgiving time, their happiness level has descended back to 7.

So how does this happen? They thought that they were on the top of the world, and they were with the five million dollars, and life has returned to normal: Richard in the clothing store, Michelle socializing with the elite of Davenport, Chris in middle school and Emma making lots of girl friends and boy friends. They all still have a relatively happy life, but it is no longer at the level of 10. Even winning the lottery doesn't necessarily make you extremely happy, except at the beginning. Thus, lots of money doesn't necessarily make you happy in the long run.

The same is true about awesome stuff. I forgot to tell you that Richard bought a Tesla for himself and one for Michelle. You can imagine how much happiness it brought them for the first several months of owning these top of the line automobiles, and, after all, they are just cars that take you from one place to another.

When we bought a new Honda at the beginning of 2020, I wasn't as happy about it as my wife. Maybe I went up a point for a week or two, and now, for me, it is just transportation. I would often just choose to drive the 2003 Infiniti instead of the Honda except for the fact that the Honda is a hybrid vehicle and is more climate-sensitive. Our happiness came back to normal, mostly because of Covid-19.

Ah yes, we also have to talk about true love. There are a number of stories I can tell you about this and the one that sticks out for me is the story of Jessica, my youngest and Vincenzo, her now husband. Before I tell this story, I need to point out that not all "true love" stories end the way Jessica's does. People, like me, think that once they find true love, they will be totally happy till death do us part. However, in truth, true love is more often a pure fantasy and should not be counted on for happiness forever. The fallacy with true love is that we come to get used to our partners, and, even though the love is still there, true life interferes. Babies are born, jobs are lost and won. Parents and grandparents become seriously ill or pass away and the children we love so much go off to college, get married and move away. So true love also fades back to normal levels of happiness, be they 7 or 8 on the scale.

The part of Jessica's story that I did not tell before is that after completing her masters' degree at the University of Barcelona, it looked like she would have to take some more courses to remain in Barcelona. She began studying Catalan, the official language of Catalonia, the region around Barcelona. Then, by fortunate circumstances, a friend introduced her to Vincenzo who was a year behind her at the University of Barcelona and they fell in love. A month before her student visa expired they were married in a civil ceremony on August 9, 2016 in Trani, Italy. They are still happily married today.

Many young women of Jessica's age and younger are so worried about having the perfect body illustrated in high culture magazines that they drive themselves down the scale of happiness. They are too fat or too skinny or too tall or too short or don't meet other standards set by high fashion models. The point is that they shouldn't be concerned about these high standards. For one, they can never meet them. For another, ultimately it will cause them a lot of suffering, especially if they have eating disorders or other compulsions. As we will see later on in the book, accepting the body that they have is a giant step away from suffering.

Other areas where misconceptions about happiness arise is in the area of "awesome stuff," "true love," and "perfect body." We think that owning awesome stuff such as a Mercedes-Benz, a country home, a yacht or a jet are going to make us happy.

However the truth is that initially, they will make us happy, and we will enjoy them from time to time, and, after a while, our happiness level will come back to normal, that is, to the level just before we made the decision to buy awesome stuff. This also plays into the "If only ..." mind that I described before. "If only I had a Mercedes-Benz, I would be happy." "If only I had a country home on Maui, I would be happy." "If only I could spend the summers on my yacht, I would be happy." "If only I could fly my own jet would I be happy."

It turns out that awesome stuff really doesn't make us happier. There was a study that showed the average happiness in the 1940s was 7.5 out of 10, whereas the average happiness in 2015 with awesome stuff, with iPhones, computers, and TV, was down to 7.2 out of 10. I grew up in the 1940s and the only way I could follow baseball was to listen to games on the radio. There was no TV or instant replay or any of the high tech gadgets that we see today. Also I would play on the swing in the back yard rather than surfing the net.

One summer day when I was about five, I was face down on the swing with my belly on the board and just appreciating the gentle motion. The sun was shining and the two other younger kids were in the house. As I swung there, I felt so calm, relaxed and happy. All of a sudden, I seemed to disappear as a person and become one with everything that was. This was my first hint of interbeing and the first spiritual experience of my life which, together with several others, have led me on the spiritual path. I knew that there was a role for me in the world and that I would survive all the suffering that ensued during my school days.

Research has also discovered that thinking about awesome stuff seems to lower our level of happiness. I know that this seems counter intuitive, and the research showed that people with a materialist attitude had less satisfaction as compared to non-materialists two decades later. The materialists even were shown to have more mental health disorders. Thus seeking out awesome stuff makes us less happy.

You will be surprised to learn that "true love" doesn't always make for lasting happiness. When I was in college and graduate school, I thought for sure having a beautiful girlfriend who would eventually become my wife, I would be happy. This developed out of an interest I had in popular music, rock and roll, and singers like Frank Sinatra all of which made me long for "true love." When it came in my last year at the University of Chicago, it was accompanied by "true suffering." Our happiness lasted about two or three years, but we were both very insecure and our marriage failed badly.

Studies show that married people are happier for about one to two years but after that, their happiness is on a par with non-married people. Average life satisfaction for women returns to normal after peaks of happiness about two years before and after a marriage.

Another surprising study of obese individuals who were followed for four years after a diet program showed that having the "perfect body" did not result in increased happiness. The individuals were placed in three groups: those that gained weight, those that lost weight and those that stayed the same. It turned out that all three groups had a drop in their happiness. Cosmetic surgery seems to have the same results as weight loss.

WHAT IS BEHIND OUR MISCONCEPTIONS?

One reason people think that what is behind the misconceptions is that some people are genetically destined to be unhappy. Another reason is that shit happens and it messes up our lives. In fact, these two answers are wrong! They only account for 60% of our general level of happiness. Our intentions, thoughts and actions account for the other 40% and they can be developed in the ways that you will learn in this book. They are under our control and mindfulness can really help us with being present for whatever arises to lead us to our true happiness.

The misconceptions that we have about how to be happy can be attributed to the annoying features of the mind that lead us astray from our true happiness called Affective Forecasting. One of these features is that our mind's strongest intuitions are often totally wrong. This occurs in situations like what lane will get me to the city the fastest or what checkout line will get me home the fastest. We are always getting these intuitions and most of the time, they are wrong. The mind delivers to us things that are factually incorrect and we mistakenly take them to be correct.

In general, for most people, our predictions about how happy something is going to make us are less good than we think, while predictions about something bad are in most cases less bad than we think. This is a manifestation of our wrong intuitions about how something is going to turn out.

I fell into this trap just after I got my cancer diagnosis in 1997. I was on my way to a friend's house after visiting the urologist when we passed the tennis courts where I would frequently play. I felt tears swelling up in my eyes and felt that the diagnosis was going to prevent me from playing tennis. I was completely wrong about this intuition and I managed to continue playing tennis into my 80s and I may be able to pick it up again.

Another annoying feature of the mind is that we tend to think in relative terms instead of absolute terms. This is called "social comparison" – a salient (but often irrelevant) standard against which all subsequent information is compared.

We set up reference points to compare our situation to that of other people and we either feel good that we have more than others or feel bad if we have less than others. This comparing mind has been discussed above when I wrote about the judging mind. Judgment plays a big role on how we use reference points and compare ourselves to others. When we do this, no matter the outcome, we suffer. We suffer because we are asking things to be different from how they actually are.

So at this point in the conversation, you might be wondering why our expectations are so bad. You have read about the first annoying feature of the mind, and here is the definition from Professor Laurie Santos who taught the most successful course ever at Yale University on *The Science of Happiness*. She defines the first feature as, "Our minds' strongest intuitions are often totally wrong."

You have also read that the second annoying feature of the mind is that our minds tend to think of things in terms relative to reference points that are usually outside of ourselves. We saw this above with the comparing mind.

There are two more really annoying features of the mind: our minds are built to get used to things, called "perceptual adaptation," and we don't realize that our minds don't get used to things. This is also called, "hedonic adaptation" – "the process of becoming accustomed to a positive or negative stimulus such that stimuli are attenuated over time."

This is what happened to my wife. Two years ago, we were forced to buy a new car because our 2003 Nissan Maxima was in the throes of dying. We didn't want to be stuck with a worthless car so we offered it to the local PBS station and got a small write off from it. We test drove a lot of cars including a Tesla and ultimately decided on a Honda Accord Hybrid. My wife was really excited about this because of all the exciting technological features they show us. However, does she use these technological features? Hardly ever, and clearly only when I'm in the car to instruct her. To quote Daniel Gilbert, PhD,

> *Wonderful things are especially wonderful the first time they happen, but their wonderfulness wanes with repetition.*

The fact that we don't realize that our minds get used to things gives rise to inaccurate predictions on what is really going to make us happy. Also, when bad things happen, we don't realize that we are not going to be that much affected by them. Just remember the example of my cancer diagnosis would mean the end of tennis for me. Things are never as bad as we think nor as good as we think because of these annoying features of the mind. Daniel Gilbert calls this "impact bias" – "the tendency to overestimate the emotional impact of a future event both in terms of intensity and its duration." "We frequently mispredict the intensity of our reactions," according to Professor Santos, and we also mispredict how long they will affect us. It turns out that our minds are more impacted toward negative things than positive things. For example, my cancer didn't turn out as bad as I thought it would because I'm still alive after more than twenty-five years of living with it. Thus, impact bias is worse for things that we don't want.

Dan Gilbert studied why we are so bad at predicting how we will feel when things happen to us and he came up with two terms that can help us cope with impact bias. The first term is called "focalism" – "the tendency to think about one event and forget about other things that happen." Focalism causes us to only think about the one bad thing that is happening to us without regard to other things that are happening in our lives. This causes us to mispredict how unhappy we are going to be.

As an example, when I was focalized on my cancer, I was ignoring what was going on with my son and twelve and fourteen year old daughters and how they were reacting to it. However, once I realized this, I dropped my predictions and began relating to the children as their father, not as a cancer patient. This played out five months later when Rachael moved on to middle school. At the moving on ceremony, she expressed her love for me and the certainty that I would survive.

The second term that Dan Gilbert coined is "immune neglect" – "unawareness of the tendency to adapt to and cope with negative events." This relates to the statement by Dr. Rick Hanson, a well-known Buddhist, psychologist and author in conversation with David Treleaven,

> Also recognizing that the brain ... has what they call a negativity bias. It's like Velcro for bad experiences, but Teflon for good ones. We're biased toward negative learning and basically, we're good at learning from bad experiences, but bad at learning from good experiences. Even though learning from good experiences of psychological resources is the primary way to heal and grow and develop and have more to offer to other people. I'm using good and bad pragmatically, as useful and beneficial.

When we recognize these effects, we are in a better place and we become more resilient. It turns out that we are actually more resilient than we think. Even though we don't like bad things to happen, we have a lot of resources for dealing with them. When we don't take advantage of these resources, we get lost in the story and descend into the "trance of unworthiness."

So how do we get over these annoying features of the mind? How do we accommodate our tendency towards miswanting? How do we use our intuition wisely instead of often being entirely wrong? How do we begin to drop our tendency to judge ourselves with respect to what other people have that we don't? How do we get used to things that we really like? And how do we get over the fact that we are built to get used to things? This is what Chapter 4 is all about: Happiness for Life!

But first, we must investigate how to reset our reference points: how we compare ourselves with respect to other people. These comparisons can show us in a good light or bad light and the change from one comparison to another. Your car is better than mine because it is a Tesla, and my care is better than yours because I practice gratitude and generosity. These reference points are affecting our happiness all the time and we don't even realize it most of the time. They are unconscious judgments that creep in when we least expect them and they affect how we live our lives and how happy we are. These comparisons invade our unconscious mind with respect to food, TV, sports and most of all social media.

So, how do we reset our reference points? One way is to re-experience what your reference point was before. Reminding us of how our lives have changed can help us reset our reference points. As an example of this, I lost a very good job in 2002 due to massive layoffs in the high tech industry and the war resulting from 911. I thought this was the worst thing that could happen so I went to job training sessions and met a friend. We started an online business of real estate referrals. I wrote all the code and he designed and did all the marketing. Then in 2004, the real estate market crashed and we were out of business. Then I learned of the Technical Committee of the Department of Justice which was looking for network protocol experts to validate Microsoft documents for accuracy as part of the settlement agreement between Microsoft and the Department of Justice. I was the first engineer hired by this committee and pulled off a brilliant solution to validate one of the Microsoft protocols. Using this technique, I was able to demonstrate that Microsoft had at least 18 errors just in the setup of the protocol. Once this was revealed to Microsoft and the DOJ, more than 50 additional engineers were hired to work on the 250 or so documents. I was now in a much better situation than when I was at the high tech company and created many more jobs for other engineers!

No more mourning about leaving the high tech company. When I thought about my situation with the high tech firm, where I had worked hard for seven years, there was no more need to compare my new job with my old one. By the way, this job with the Technical Committee ended in 2011 and it was my final full time position. My reference point about jobs was permanently reset!

The counter of this is to concretely observe a different reference point, like having no job at all. This can help you to see the futility of reference points. Remember, "To desire what you don't have is to waste what you do have!" This relates directly to the "If only..." mind of the second chapter. Then you can reset your reference point or not have one at all.

Since the worst kinds of reference points are other people, we can learn to avoid social comparisons altogether. One way I have done this is to avoid social media. Even though I still have all my social media accounts (Facebook, Instagram, Twitter, Pinterest, ...) I only pay attention to them on very rare occasions. For example, if one of my children points me to something they thought I'd be interested in. Just today, Jessica sent me a reference to how whales sequester significantly more carbon dioxide than trees and I found it intriguing.

When you find yourself in a moment of comparison, you can use the stop technique from cognitive behavioral therapy. I think this works for me when I see young people having a great time eating together, chatting and having a good time. I can, at times, wallow in my regrets about having limited friends throughout my life. So if I apply the stop technique, I can recognize that I have all I need to be happy in the present moment and my longing will dissipate. The technique I use is "pause, relax, open". I pause for a moment, take a breath, relax into the breath and open to the present moment experience and allow it to transform me. Incidentally, gratitude practice can also be a good way to put a stop to social comparison. Gratitude is kind of a killer of jealousy and envy and we become less likely to make social comparisons.

We can also be conscious of the kinds of social comparisons we are letting in. We get some of these ideas when we watch commercials or television programs that spark our social comparison system. For me, this has the effect of abhorring commercial TV, and, for the most part, I won't watch anything on TV that has commercials. I am especially annoyed by drug commercials which make everyone think that they are unhealthy and need this new drug to be healthy and happy. This bugs the hell out of me and I refuse to let this kind of stuff into my life. The same is basically true for the news. I don't care to listen to what stupid people have done to wreck or destroy our democracy. They ought to be taken out of the daily news broadcasts.

Another way to deal with your reference points is to reduce your consumption. Remember the adage, invest in experiences not things. This basically means to have a small portion of chocolate (or your favorite snack) often rather than a large portion all at once. As you get down to the bottom of a larger portion, your happiness decreases. For example, a couple of weeks ago, we went out to dinner and I ordered lobster. The portion was much larger and much more expensive than I thought. By the time I was half way through the lobster, I was no longer hungry and I kept on eating anyway. The last portion certainly wasn't as enjoyable as the first part of the meal.

Finally, we can add variety into our lives. Rather than always eating breakfast at the same restaurant (as I tend to do when I have breakfast out), it could possibly make me happier by trying a different one from time to time. However, the fact remains, that the one I go to is the best one in town because no other restaurant makes crispy bacon as well as my favorite. Some come close, but no cigar. By the way, breakfast is my favorite meal. I offer myself some variety in my food choices there. I switch around from waffles to pancakes to pancakes with blueberries.

This also goes back to the wisdom of investing in experiences rather than things. Things tend to stay around more and we can become bored with them. Experiences can be varied from day to day, week to week, etc. For example, I plan to do a walking meditation every day. If I went on the same path every day, it would get ultimately boring, so I try to choose a different path each day. On my walk, I sometimes pass people, and, in most cases, I will offer a "G'day" or "Hello" and when they pass, I wish them well.

The last topic we have to address before going into *Happiness for Life* (chapter 4), is to deal with overcoming biases. Remember, often, our strongest intuitions are often completely wrong.

PRACTICE WITH MISWANTING

Now that we've covered all the annoying features of the mind, how do we practice with miswanting? Here is what I invite you to do.

Step 1:
We begin by taking six deep breaths. When you breathe in..., breathe in completely and deeply..., filling your chest and abdomen as fully as possible... When you breathe out..., simply let go of all the air and the tensions you are holding... [Repeat a minimum of three to six times.]

Breathe in completely and deeply... Hold your breath for a count of three... Let go and release all the air in your lungs...

Breathe in deeply again... Hold for a count of three... Let go...

Breathe in again to your full capacity... Hold for a count of three... Breathe out and release...

In... in... in... One... Two... Three... Out... out... out...

Breathe in deeply again... Hold for a count of three... Let go...

Breathe in again to your full capacity... Hold for a count of three... Breathe out and release...

Now discontinue breathing deeply... and allow your breath to naturally return to normal... Take your time... Take it easy...

Step 2:

Now that your breathing has become normal... Withdraw yourself... into yourself... Become aware of your body... Notice how your body is connected to the earth... Open your senses... Taste inside your mouth and on your lips... The smell of air coming in your nostrils... Notice the ambient sounds... Don't become attached to them... Let them go... And sight... Eyes resting... insight opening... investigation opening... imagination opening... And touch... Notice your feet and legs... Notice your hips and pelvis... Notice your abdomen and lower back... Notice your rib cage and middle back... Notice your chest and upper back... Be aware of your shoulders... On down to your arms, hands and fingers... Notice your neck and the back of your head... Notice your face...

Continue to breathe naturally...

[Now continue being aware of your body until you are ready to move on.]

Be aware... of no other spaces... but these spaces...

Be aware... of no other times... but these times...

Be here... Be now... Be here, now...

Step 3:

Now bring to mind something that you think you desire to be happy right now. It could be almost anything from a new shirt or blouse to a Tesla. Notice how you feel in your body when you think about this item. Ask yourself, "What about this item is going to make me happier?" What do you feel in your body when you ask this question? Do you actually feel happy or do you feel anxious? Just notice.

Step 4:

Now ask yourself, "Why is this item going to make me happier? Notice the reaction to this question in your body. Do you feel any different from Step 3? If so, what is the difference? Where do you feel it in your body? How do you feel about the item of your desire right now? Just notice.

Step 5:

Now ask yourself, "How is this item going to make me happier?" What do you feel now in your body? Has anything changed? If so, what is the difference? Can you now explain what, why and how this item is going to make you happy? Then, ask yourself, "Is this item still so important to me?" If so, happy shopping. If not, let the desire for the item fade away just as a cloud disappears as it moves across the sky. In either case, your miswanting has been dealt with, whether you buy the item or not.

How was this practice for you? Did you learn anything? Were you able to notice how miswanting can cause us a lot of suffering? You may want to write the answers to these questions in your journal.

CHAPTER 4: HAPPINESS FOR LIFE

In this chapter, we will explore what increases our happiness. It is based on Buddhist principles as well as scientific studies on happiness. From the point of view of science, we will explore methods to overcome the misconceptions and biases in how our minds function and relate them to how to use mindfulness to be happy. We will develop strategies that we can use to overcome miswanting awesome things. To make things better, we have to want to change our outlook on the things we think will make us happy. Sonja Lyumbormirsky, a professor at the University of California, Riverside writes,

> *"Our intentional, effortful activities have a powerful effect on how happy we are, over and above the effects of our set points and the circumstances in which we find ourselves."*

So we must have a strong intention to change if we are to obtain any degree of happiness for life. With these tools, we can overcome hedonic adaptation, which keeps us looped into wanting awesome things. We learned that hedonic adaptation means that we get used to things and the things that we buy remain the same for a long time until their useful life expires. And, they no longer make us happy once they are sitting around in our garage!

HEDONIC ADAPTATION

The first step in this strategy to counteract hedonic adaptation is to stop buying things. The point is not to invest in things that are going to wind up in the garage in the long run. They only bring us momentary happiness. We think these things are going to really make us happy, and they don't. They stick around for a short or long time and we just get used to having them around. We often get bored with them and want to replace them with newer shiny objects that we think are better. Dan Gilbert says,

> *"Part of us believes the new car is better because it lasts*

> longer. But in fact that's the worst thing about the new car... It will stay around to disappoint you."

This is and was certainly true for our new Honda, with all of its electronic and advanced features. I still prefer to drive the 2003 Infiniti G35!

So if we are not investing in things like cars, boats and computers, what should we invest in? Well, one thing that I have learned primarily from my daughter, Jessica, is to invest in experiences. Somehow, she learned this lesson very early in life and now, living in Barcelona for the past nine years, she walks the talk. She won't even wear a wedding ring or wear much jewelry. She doesn't want to inherit my wife's extensive jewelry collection, even to put it on the market for sale. If you ask her if she wants a new computer or a trip to Israel, she will definitely opt for the latter.

We can learn to invest in experiences like visiting an art gallery, taking a hike in the woods, traveling to an exotic place, having good food with friends in a restaurant, playing a sport like tennis, going to a concert or whatever pleases you. These are valuable simply because it allows us a chance for social connection and provides opportunities for us to share about our experiences. Here's more from Dan Gilbert:

> "A new car sticks around to disappoint you. But a trip to Europe is over. It evaporates. It has the good sense to go away, and you are left with nothing but a wonderful memory."

And, as I already mentioned, you can share the experience with your family and friends. When people think about buying a new car or spending time on vacation, their happiness ratings seem to favor going on vacation. They are happier about thinking about their vacation. They also think that the trip contributes more to their happiness and the vacation is money well spent.

It turns out that just thinking about taking a nice trip can enhance our level of happiness and reduce our tendency for hedonic adaptation. For example, my wife and I have enjoyed trips to Carmel, California since the late 1970s, when we could get a room for $25 per night! We are now planning a trip there as I write this section and it would cost us now $727, and it is going to be paid for by a friend, Barbara. When one of my best friends, Philip, died in April in Coral Gables, Florida, 2022, just before his 93rd birthday, his wife, the donor of our trip, wanted to check out of their summer apartment in Mill Valley, California and my wife took the leading role in distributing their things in the apartment. Mala did things out of love for Barbara and Philip and Barbara wanted to reward her.

So, even before we go to Carmel, we are experiencing a sweet amount of happiness that no possession could provide. Our anticipation is high and this contributes to our happiness. We look forward to walking in Point Lobos, visiting China Beach and the Bird Rock, walking on Carmel Beach and the beautiful shops and restaurants that Carmel has to offer. We've been going there so long that it is now only the restaurants that I am interested in. I think Mala will likely shop a little while I nap in our room at the Wayside Inn.

Thus, even though we don't adapt very well to experiences, they can make us happier than things. This has been borne out by scientific experiments where subjects thought they would be much happier buying something rather than an experience. However, two to four weeks after buying something or investing in an experience, their happiness levels were significantly higher with the experience than the thing that they bought. The problem is that we don't seem to realize that the experience would gain us more happiness.

The fact that experiences are better than purchasing things leads to other benefits. For example, when you tell people about your experiences, they get a little taste of your experience and they feel happy too. The people you tell will likely respond by co-regulating with you, that is, they will pick up on your happiness with the experience. This is totally borne out by the life my daughter lives in Barcelona. In a single day, she can paddle board in the morning, visit friends in the afternoon for lunch, go to an

Italian theater production and later go to a barbeque in the evening, as she did on the day I wrote this paragraph.

It's important to note that experiences are more difficult to apply our comparing mind to than things. It's pretty easy to judge whether your BMW is superior to my 2003 Infiniti or my 2020 Honda Accord Hybrid. But how could you compare my experience of China Beach in Point Lobos State Reserve to your experience of Baker Beach in San Francisco? It just wouldn't make any sense. Thus, experiences are less influenced by social comparison than things.

Other techniques for thwarting hedonic adaptation include savoring, negative visualization, making this day your last and gratitude. Savoring and gratitude will come later in chapter 5.

NEGATIVE VISUALIZATION

So what is negative visualization? Negative visualization is the process of thinking about how our lives would be different if certain things hadn't happened. This can help you break out of hedonic adaptation. For example, I asked myself what would have happened if I had never assumed custody of my son after his mother forced him to take two buses and two and one-half hours to travel to where she was living in Lake County every single weekend, come rain or come shine.

This rigid schedule had an adverse effect on my son and would have continued until she had some sense to do something good for him. It is possible that if Micah had lived with his mother in a friendly neighborhood in San Francisco instead of a commune in Lake County, Mala and I would not have needed to get custody. Then, she might not have seen what a good father I was to him and she may not have wanted to marry me. If all of this happened, the girls would not have been born and my life would not be the same.

You might want to take out a piece of paper and write for fifteen minutes about how you might not have met your partner. This is the exercise that I just did in the previous paragraph. People who did this in a research project had a higher level of overall happiness than people who just wrote about how they met their partner.

We can also think about losing something to thwart hedonic adaptation. For example, if you are about to change jobs, move to a new city, buy a different house or retire, thinking about your future allows good things to pop up. Maybe you'll be taking a vacation before your next job or thinking that your new house has many advantages over where you are currently living can induce a degree of happiness in you. This is similar to negative visualization and is called making this day your last. Thinking about losing something is a good way out of hedonic adaptation.

MANAGING REFERENCE POINTS

Now let's turn to reference points and how we compare ourselves and what we have to others. You may recall that reference points are relative to how we judge things. If I'm making $50,000 per year and you are making $60,000 per year and we are doing similar kinds of work, I would certainly judge myself to be less than you and perhaps do less work to compensate for the salary difference. This totally leaves out whether or not I like my job or that it has other benefits. I am judging myself to the reference point of your $60,000 salary. My reference point to your salary is measured against an almost irrelevant standard. I am not looking to an absolute standard for this comparison so it is very emotional and has no effect on how good the job actually is for me.

It is much better for me to look for a job which magnifies and utilizes my signature strengths for concentration, presence, and moral fortitude than to find one with a lot of money. Although, with the Technical Committee, I had both a job that utilized my strengths and paid me good money. Signature strength can be characterized as desires or disposition to act, or a feeling that involves the exercise of judgment that leads to a recognizable human excellence or instance of human flourishing. You might want to stop for a moment and list what you think your signature strengths are in your journal or other recording mechanism.

CHARACTER STRENGTHS

Signature strengths, also known as character strengths, seem to be ubiquitous, that is, widely recognized across cultures; fulfilling, like my job with the Technical Committee; valued ethically; and tend not to diminish others. These strengths tend to be stable in an individual forming a character trait. Signature strengths seem to be distinctive from other strengths. They lead to a good deal of virtue such as humor, love, kindness, gratitude, creativity, integrity and others. Using our signature strengths in our jobs and in our lives has the effect of increasing our overall happiness. To continue with the Technical Committee story, we would meet once a week in Palo Alto for status reports, assignments and the like and we were able to develop a lot of good social connections, which we will look at later. Using my signature strengths caused my productivity to go up along with my job satisfaction.

Oftentimes, during my tenure with the Technical Committee I would find myself in a state of flow, which means that I was fully immersed in a feeling of energized focus, full involvement and enjoyment. This is just like being "in the zone," as many athletes have suggested a reason for their tremendous performance. It can happen at work too, if we are in a meaningful job. In flow, you can easily lose track of time, as I often did with my work. You can also have feelings of serenity and loss of self-consciousness. One flow researcher, Mihaly Csikszentmihalyi, put it this way,

> "The best moments in our lives are not the passive, receptive, relaxing ones. The best moments really occur when a person's body and mind is stretched to its limits in a voluntary effort to accomplish something difficult and worthwhile."

I'd say that this is what happened to me when I was teaching the courses upon which this book is based. If you review the recordings, you may be able to pick this out from certain of the classes, especially the class on sympathetic joy (chapter 8). It also happens to me when I prepare for my weekly sangha.

SOCIAL CONNECTION

The comradery I experienced with the people in the Technical

Committee was an example of social connection, which has been found to be one of the most significant things to increase happiness. I also experience this when my family is around and when I spend time with friends. Unfortunately, I did not experience much social connection when I was younger and now I recognize what I have missed. All of this changed when Mala and I got together. She had a circle of friends that became my friends and I'm still happy to be alone.

Social connection has been shown to have a bunch of health benefits as well as happiness benefits. For example, people with close relationships are less vulnerable to premature death and are able to cope with stressful events. They are also less likely to succumb to a fatal illness. For example, my son survived metastatic kidney cancer which presented in 1976. When we took him to the doctor four years later, we were told that he was the first child to survive his type of kidney cancer ever documented by doctors. The key to his remarkable recovery was, in my opinion, a result of the use of "mind stories" – guided meditations for children – which I taught him in the hospital and which continued with Dr. Sheldon Ruderman. You can see Micah's story at mindfulnessinhealing.org.

My cancer story has had a similar outcome. I was diagnosed with muscle invasive bladder cancer in 1997. I immediately took charge of my own healing experience by doing research and knowing my probable diagnosis before being told by Dr. Neuwirth. I applied myself to mindfulness and meditation and continue the practices to this day. I investigated alternatives, made lifestyle changes, wisely chose a medical team, attended support groups and gave back to my community. See *Healing Cancer with Your Mind: 7 Strategies to Help YOU Survive*, for more details.

Psychologists have found that people with close friends, strong family ties and a healthy romance tend to rate their happiness higher than others. In their daily activities, they enjoy spending time with their family and friends. It turns out that even finding social connections with strangers can increase your happiness as well as the happiness of the stranger. So it pays to "reach out and touch someone!" Even today, when I was doing my walking meditation in Sausalito, I practiced saying, "Hello!" to the strangers I encountered. There were plenty of people (some in costumes because of Halloween) who responded and it made me happy. I think it made them happy too!

Nicolas Epley, a prominent social scientist from the University of Chicago says,

> Social connection can be almost anything, from making eye contact with another person, or smiling at another person to being in a long term romantic relationship with somebody. And it turns out that, social connection across this entire spectrum, tends to be pretty darn good for people. Or another way of saying that is the absence of social connection, social isolation, tends to be pretty awful for people.

He thinks that just seeking out social connection can make a difference. I think that it explains what I experience when I do my walking meditation and make sure to say "Hello," or wave to a passerby. It marks a social connection for me and the person who responds. Sometimes, I get criticized for doing this by my wife. She has plenty of social connections and, I guess, doesn't need this one and doesn't think others need it also.

Epley also reports that an experience of loneliness on happiness is seven times bigger that a fourfold increase of income! So it is really important to connect with lonely people and could they possibly be the ones I pass on the path of my walking meditation?

TIME AFFLUENCE

There are a few other areas to explore to increase happiness in your life. Did you know that people who prioritize time over money are happier than people who prioritize money over time? Are you someone who would gladly sacrifice money to have more quality time with your children, your spouse, your extended family and your friends? Or are you someone who wants money more than anything in my life? We were looking for a house to buy in 1998, a year after the onset of my cancer. We looked at this house in Mill Valley and I spoke to the owner. I asked him what he wanted out of life and all he could say was money. The conversation stopped right then and there. We did not buy his house. Researchers found that people who valued time over money were happier than people who focused on money even though more than two-thirds of the people in the survey valued money over time. So, prioritizing time over money has the effect of generating more happiness.

CONTROLLING OUR MINDS

As you are reading this book, are you really reading it with your full attention or are the words just passing from the book to your eyes? Do you easily get distracted when you are reading? I am certainly guilty of this to a strong degree and I am getting much better as my meditation practice improves.

The problem is that our minds are made that way. They are easily distracted by just about anything. How do we stop our minds from being all over the place? How do we get our minds to stick to the task that we assigned to them? Psychologists call this *mind-wandering*:

> ...a shift in the contents of thought away from an ongoing task and/or from events in the external environment to self-generated thoughts and feelings, often to things that are in the past or in the future. Scientists have found that our minds wander almost half of the time!

This is actually a feature of the neuroscience of our brain. You probably know that various parts of the brain perform different tasks. For example, there are parts of the brain that recognize faces. Other parts of the brain are used for language and speaking. There are also the visual and auditory cortexes in the brain for sight and hearing. In addition, there is a network in the brain that seems to operate all the time when we are not active. This is called the *default network*: A network of interacting brain regions known to activate "by default" when a person is not involved in a task. This network kicks in when we are not doing any specific task like listening or talking or seeing. It seems to be the most efficient state for the brain to be in when it is not working on something specific. The different regions of the brain that constitute the default network can come on really fast – in less than a fraction of a second! They are also responsible for getting us out of the here and now and moving into the past or the future or something else.

Is this mind wandering effect of the default network really good? There don't seem to be other species that have the capability to think about the past or plan for the future. Is this really good? One research study sampled a couple of thousand people by pinging them at random times asking them, "What are you doing? Are you thinking about what you're doing now?" and other questions including, "Are you happy?" They found out that people are mind-wandering a little less than fifty percent of the time of their waking hours. They also found that people mind-wander about thirty percent of the time in almost all activities when they are supposed to be focused except for sex. They also found that mind-wandering had a negative effect on their happiness. The results also showed that people who were thinking about the upcoming vacation or meeting a nice person at a party, their happiness did not fall. Dan Gilbert, one of the scientists on this project and author of *Stumbling on Happiness* said,

> "The ability to think about what is not happening is a cognitive achievement that comes at an emotional cost."
> "A wandering mind is an unhappy mind."

So how do we stop this wandering mind? You must know by now that one way to do this is mindfulness meditation. I think that the neuroscience explanation of mind-wandering will help you to make a commitment to a daily practice of nine minutes a day. It is all right to split it into a four minute practice and a five minute practice – whatever suits your schedule. Meditation is a way of turning your attention away from distracting thoughts towards what is called an anchor: the breath in the belly or chest or nostrils, body sensations, loving kindness (chapter 6), compassion (chapter 7), or even the contemplation of a specific teaching such as impermanence or the end of suffering. This will help you to stop your mind from wandering, and the more you practice, the more benefit you will get.

In addition to meditation, exercise and sleep have been shown to have benefits just like meditation. For example, exercising for thirty minutes a day for three times each week was shown to produce better results than taking Zoloft or taking Zoloft with exercising. You don't need Zoloft if you are exercising regularly. It also works really well for elderly people to exercise as long as they are capable.

Sleeping about seven to eight hours of sleep at night has shown to make people happier in scientific studies. Sleeping has other benefits like increasing your performance at work or whatever tasks you need to accomplish. I have found that taking naps in the afternoon after my walking meditation keeps me awake and alert well into the night. When I don't nap, I find myself going to bed earlier and not getting enough sleep.

Research has shown that after one night of insufficient sleep (five hours or less), you may show signs of being hungrier and eating more, you are more likely to have an accident, you may be losing some brain tissue, you are more likely to catch a cold, you are more likely to get emotional, you become less focused and have difficulty remembering things, and, probably worst of all, you are more likely not to look your best. Chronic sleep deprivation can be even much worse. You become more at risk for strokes, obesity, certain cancers, diabetes, heart disease and death. A man's sperm count can also go down with lack of sleep.

PRACTICE WITH HAPPINESS FOR LIFE

We now come to the practice of happiness for life. We've seen how all the topics in this chapter have the effect of increasing our happiness for life. Now we need to practice with them on a daily basis and the way to do this is to have an appropriate goal aiming at a happy life. This practice is about how to accomplish your goals using a mindfulness meditation practice on a daily basis. Note: this practice first appeared in my recording of *Achieve Goals Guided Meditation* and then again in my book, *Mindfulness Breaks: Your Path to Awakening*.

Gratitude, loving kindness and forgiveness are the true foundations for a life of love and happiness. As you will see in a later chapter, these contribute vastly to inner peace, tranquility and equanimity. These qualities purify your heart and mind and promote beneficial hormones in your brain. These are some things to strive for and meditate upon on a daily basis. When gratitude, loving kindness and forgiveness are in place, it is much, much easier to accomplish your goals, whatever they might be.

Are you looking for a partner to share your life with? Are you looking for a new place to live or a new job? Do you need to figure out what to do with a health condition? Is your home or car in bad need of repair? Do you want to start a business of your own? Father Eli taught that this type of meditation is a wonderful tool for achieving goals.

In life, it is necessary to have some sort of goal. It might be as simple as getting up each day and going off to work so you can chill on the weekend. It might be earning enough money to retire early in life and play golf or tennis every day. Whatever your goal is, it is what you are trying to achieve. You'll find that most successful people have well defined goals.

Some people maintain to-do lists. Many times, things get skipped over and never accomplished. A to-do list is fine if you follow through. Setting goals outside of your to-do list can help you achieve them as long as you diligently pursue them.

People talk about *The Secret*, a book and documentary that tells you that whatever you believe and conceive you can achieve. What they don't tell you is that the people they interviewed worked diligently to achieve their goals. They were not deterred from them when things didn't go their way. They continued to pursue their goals with hard work and diligence. There is no substitute for hard work when it comes to achieving your goals.

Father Eli taught us to aim high! We should not settle for anything less than what we want. He says,

"Be sure to make your goals high enough. If one jumps for the highest limb possible, he can always catch a lower one on his way down."

We shouldn't have too many goals. Think of the child who wants so many toys that he can't choose one to be satisfied with. In the beginning, we should choose three goals. The first goal should be a short-range goal to be completed in about three to six months. This goal should be relatively easy to obtain, for example, a new job, home or iPhone. The second one should be a mid-range goal of perhaps three to five years in the future. This should pertain to something in your life that you would like to improve such as your relationship with your parents or children, or better and more loving friendships, or a new home, or a trip around the world. The third type of goal should be a lifetime achievement goal such as awakening, perfection, or simply peace of mind.

To clarify your goals, take a plain piece of paper and divide it into three columns. In the first column, write "Ten things I'd like to do." In the second column, write "Ten things I'd like to own." In the third column, write "Ten things I'd like to change in myself." Now select the easiest one to work on from the top of the three columns and focus on it.

Now that you have chosen the goal that you want to work on, you must realize that there may be several things that you may have to do to accomplish your goal. So, for example, if you want to cook a nice meal for your spouse, you would need to decide what to cook, obtain the ingredients, consult a recipe, make sure you have the right utensils, etc. On another piece of paper, write down the goal that you want to achieve. On the next line, write down "The time limit is..." and fill in the blank. Having a specified time limit is very important to keep you on track to your goal. We accomplish them by overcoming obstacles and weaknesses, not by praying, visualizing or talking about them. We need to enumerate these obstacles and weaknesses in order to have a chance to accomplish our goals.

On the left side of the paper, write "Things I must overcome," and on the right side of the paper, write "What I'm going to do about it." Ask yourself, "Which one am I going to do first?" Sometimes, it is important to do these tasks in sequence and sometimes the tasks can be done independently. Using the example of the meal from above, you may have certain ingredients in your home and don't have to put them on your shopping list. Extending this a little, you may already have all the utensils you need, but not have a critical ingredient like the fish you want to fry or the oil you want to fry it in.

The hardest thing about goal setting and execution is knowing how to begin. The goal practice can help you figure out what the best way for you to begin. Not only that, by getting a clear picture of your goal and the steps needed to accomplish it, it may become easier to obtain.

Before you begin this practice for achieving your goals, you should have your objective clearly in mind; along with a feeling for the obstacles you must overcome to achieve it. Goals should be specific. For example, if you are going to begin a mindfulness meditation practice, you should ask yourself, "How am I going to meditate? Where? Here in my house or with a group of people (called a *sangha*). What time will I meditate? Will I do it every day or x times a week? How long am I going to meditate?" For me, my morning meditation begins within 10 minutes of waking up and I practice a minimum of twenty minutes daily. Exercise and shower usually follow meditation. Later in the day, I most likely do walking meditation outside on public paths and at night, I complete with gratitude meditation. Specifying the length of time you will meditate is really beneficial. I recommend beginning with only nine minutes a day at any time you desire. Basically, figuring out how you are going to meditate sets the stage for implanting a new habit of meditation.

Goals should also be time specific. For example, my goal to have this book completed by the end of 2022 gives me a time-specific goal to achieve. People often set unrealistic goals without being time-specific and then they never accomplish them.

Another example related to achieving goals took place in my life in 1973. I had spent the summer on retreat with Father Eli in the Arkansas Ozark Mountains. When the retreat ended, I had two weeks to get to California to see my son and return to Chicago for the fall semester at Oakton Community College. There I was, lying on my ex-wife's floor doing this visualization for a job in the Bay Area. The next day, I learned of a sabbatical replacement opportunity in computer programming at the College of Marin. I applied and got the job. I still had to go back to Chicago to close up my apartment and move to the West Coast. This practice has worked flawlessly for me in several other instances, some of which you have read about in the introduction.

THE GOAL SETTING PRACTICE

Step 1:
We begin by taking six deep breaths. When you breathe in..., breathe in completely and deeply..., filling your chest and abdomen as fully as possible... When you breathe out..., simply let go of all the air and the tensions you are holding... [Repeat a minimum of three to six times.]

Breathe in completely and deeply... Hold your breath for a count of three... Let go and release all the air in your lungs...

Breathe in deeply again... Hold for a count of three... Let go...

Breathe in again to your full capacity... Hold for a count of three... Breathe out and release...

In... in... in... One... Two... Three... Out... out... out...

Breathe in deeply again... Hold for a count of three... Let go...

Breathe in again to your full capacity... Hold for a count of three... Breathe out and release...

Now discontinue breathing deeply... and allow your breath to naturally return to normal... Take your time... Take it easy...

Step 2:
Now that your breathing has become normal... Withdraw yourself... into yourself... Become aware of your body... Notice how your body is connected to the earth... Open your senses... Taste inside your mouth and on your lips... The smell of air coming in your nostrils... Notice the ambient sounds... Don't become attached to them... Let them go... And sight... Eyes resting...

insight opening... investigation opening... imagination opening... And touch... Notice your feet and legs... Notice your hips and pelvis... Notice your abdomen and lower back... Notice your rib cage and middle back... Notice your chest and upper back... Be aware of your shoulders... On down to your arms, hands and fingers... Notice your neck and the back of your head... Notice your face...

Continue to breathe naturally...

[Now continue being aware of your body until you are ready to move on.]

Be aware... of no other spaces... but these spaces...

Be aware... of no other times... but these times...

Be here... Be now... Be here, now...

Step 3:

Allow an image to form that represents the completion of your goal... Where are you? ... What do you see? ... What do you smell? ... What do you hear? ... What do you taste? ... Allow this image to become clearer... What's happening now? ... What does the scene look like from a short distance above? ... What does the scene look like from far away? ... Who is with you? ... As you ponder these questions..., allow the image to evolve... Begin to get a sense of what you have to do to get there... Take your time... Don't hurry... Don't worry about how good your image is... or whether you have a clear image at all...

Now let that image go... and think about what is going on right now... Allow an image to form that relates to the first step you must take to reach your goal... See it clearly... Where are you? ... What do you see? ... What do you smell? ... What do you hear? ... What do you taste? ... Allow this image to become clearer... What's happening now? ... What does the scene look like from a short distance above? ... What does the scene look like from far away? ... Who is with you? ... As you ponder these questions..., allow the image to evolve... Promise yourself that you will take action on this first step as soon as possible...

Now let go of this image and return to your breath... Breathing in..., know that you are breathing in... Breathing out..., know that you are breathing out... Relax... Let go... Release...

How do you feel? Now would be a good time to write down anything that occurred to you during the visualization. What insights did you have, if any? What was your end goal? What is your first step to achieving that goal? What action will you take to accomplish this first step? Note that this may simply be a planning step in which you outline all the tasks you must complete before you can accomplish your goal. Report back to me about your achievements!

A few months ago, I was on a Zoom call with a woman named Diana Hill who had made a trip with her family to Plum Village, France. She was so impressed with everything she encountered there and wrote about it in her blog, The Wise Brain Bulletin. Here is what she wrote about Happiness Is Here and Now:

> As an Acceptance and Commitment Therapy practitioner, I teach people to accept and allow for life's suffering so they can act on what matters to them. Daily living, a pandemic, racial trauma, climate change, and war give us plenty of material to work with.
> At Plum Village, I learned that cultivating joy and happiness is as important as acceptance in facing our suffering. To cultivate more joy, the nun leading our group, Sister Joyful Effort, gave us homework: we were to look for joyful moments in our day and share them with others.
> I noticed the cool shade of aspen trees on a hot walk and the sound of kids giggling during silent meditation. Sharing these joys with my family, enriched them.
> In times like these, when so many people are struggling, it can seem saccharine to talk about joy. But it is what gives us the strength to go on. We need to cultivate joy in order to have the capacity to be with the suffering, and the bigger the suffering, the more we need to cultivate joy. Savoring the good things in life builds resilience and increases our satisfaction with life. Paying attention to the joyful moments builds our capacity to be present with pain.

How to Cultivate Joy
  Look for small moments of happiness or ease.
  Savor your experience by lingering on it, paying attention to your full sensory experience.
  Hold these moments lightly and with delight.
  Share the joy by telling someone else.

CHAPTER 5: LOVING KINDNESS
THE FOUR DIVINE ABODES

The rest of this book is devoted to the teachings on the Four Divine Abodes. These are also known as the Brahmaviharas, the Sublime Abodes and the Four Immeasurable Minds. They are called divine because practicing them puts you in touch with whatever you consider divine. They are sublime because they point to the most wholesome, most loving, most affirming way of relating to ourselves and to other people. They are immeasurable because the more we practice them, the more joy and happiness they bring. They continue to grow with practice throughout our lives. According to Vanessa Zuisei Goddard, a Zen Buddhist teacher and writer,

> *The four immeasurables are variously known as the "abodes of Brahma" (brahmavihara), divine abidings, heavenly abodes, or the four sublime or excellent states. They are excellent because, in their manifestation, they are limitless. They are sublime because they point to the most wholesome, most loving, most affirming way of relating to others and ourselves.*

The Four Divine Abodes are loving kindness (*metta or maitri*), compassion (*karuna*), sympathetic joy (*mudita*) and equanimity (*upekka*). One of the founding sages of yoga, Patanjali, said,

> *Loving kindness and friendliness towards the happy, compassion for the sorrowful, joy for others and equanimity or being undisturbed by events and not being drawn into judgement or contempt are the four attitudes that will bring peace of mind.*

I came across these teachings more than twenty-five years ago and they have become the cornerstone of my practice. They are my favorite Buddhist teachings. Contemplating loving kindness, compassion, sympathetic joy and equanimity brings me much happiness. The Buddha explained the divine abodes to his son, Rahula (which means, "fetter") the following.

> The Buddha taught the following to his son Rahula
> "Rahula, practice loving kindness to overcome anger. Loving kindness has the capacity to bring happiness to others without demanding anything in return.
> Practice compassion to overcome cruelty. Compassion has the capacity to remove the suffering of others without expecting anything in return.
> Practice sympathetic joy to overcome hatred. Sympathetic joy arises when one rejoices over the happiness of others and wishes others well-being and success.
> Practice non-attachment to overcome prejudice. Non-attachment is the way of looking at all things openly and equally. This is because that is. Myself and others are not separate. Do not reject one thing only to chase after another.
> I call these the four immeasurables. Practice them and you will become a refreshing source of vitality and happiness for others." - Thich Nhat Hahn, Old path white clouds

The chart of the divine abodes that was in the magazine from the Barre Center for Buddhist Studies back in 1997, also presented pairings with an opposite state as well as a near neighbor. The near neighbors can look like the quality, but don't have a genuine feeling of it. The near neighbor of loving kindness, for example, is sentimentality, which is self-referential and has a separating quality. The opposite of loving kindness is obviously anger or ill will. Kate Johnson, one of my teachers in the MMTCP program taught this at Spirit Rock, a meditation center in Marin County, California:

> Mettā [loving kindness] is the heart of love turned towards the good qualities of ourselves or another being, and compassion is the heart of love turned towards suffering. Mudita [sympathetic joy] is the heart of love turned

towards the good fortune of others, and equanimity is the heart of love turned towards wisdom.
Equanimity is the heart of love that is able to hold the truth of suffering; the truth of change, the unfathomable workings of karma, and able to be with the fact that we're not able to control circumstances all the time. It's the heart that's able to hold all of these things and to love anyway. Equanimity is not the same as indifference. It's just love with a lot of space. That space makes it a sustainable kind of love, and one that's very useful for challenging times.

This chapter focuses on loving kindness. Each subsequent chapter will deal with the other divine abodes in turn.

LOVING KINDNESS

Cultivation of loving kindness is basically a transpersonal experience. We open ourselves up to feelings of sympathy for all sentient beings, plants and animals included. The Buddha taught this about loving kindness:

> "I will abide pervading the all-encompassing world with a mind imbued with loving-kindness, abundant, exalted, immeasurable, without hostility, and without ill will." – Subha Sutra, MN 99 [a reference to an ancient document]

Thich Nhat Hanh said it this way, "Your compassion and loving kindness are invincible and without limit."

Scientific research has shown that seeking out to perform acts of kindness does not only make us happy. It also increases the happiness of the person we are kind to. You probably know by now that I married a woman who manifests the quality of kindness in spades. For example, when my friend, Philip died last April in Coral Gables, Florida, Mala took it on herself to take care of emptying Phil and Barbara's apartment in Mill Valley, almost entirely on her own. She did it totally out of love for Barbara and Phil and out of the kindness of her heart. I have seen her do many more acts of kindness over the 40+ years of our marriage. In fact, when people ask me why I married her, I would tell them that she was the kindest person I'd ever met. Jeffrey Hopkins, an interpreter for the Dalai Lama and Buddhist translator and teacher said,

> *Kindness is Society*
> *During a lecture while I was interpreting for the Dalai Lama, he said in what seemed to me to be broken English, "Kindness is society." I wasn't smart enough to think he was saying kindness is society. I thought he meant kindness is important to society; kindness is vital to society; but he was saying that kindness is so important that we cannot have society without it. Society is impossible without it. Thus, kindness IS society; society IS kindness. Without concern for other people it's impossible to have society.*

So, simple acts of kindness are known to bring us happiness. Even thinking about or remembering kind acts which were done for you can, in some circumstances, increase happiness. Thus it pays to do random acts of kindness on a daily basis. For example, when I do walking meditation on a public path with lots of people, I make it a practice to say, "Hello," or wave to them. You would be surprised to know that most people I pass in this way light up a little, as if someone cares about how their day is going. Sometimes, I say to myself as I pass these people, "May you be free," especially if they tend to ignore my actions. I feel happy when people respond and I don't feel less happy when they don't. I recognize that they don't want to interact and may be suffering inside. That's why I wish them to be free.

Another strange finding in research studies concerns spending money on ourselves or on other people. Research in Canada and Uganda shows that people who spend money on others are happier than people who spend money on themselves when they are given money to spend by researchers by the end of the day. I think this carries over to spending money on my family. For example, twice last week we had dinner with my son, his wife and my granddaughter. Each time, when the bill came, I wound up paying for it without even asking if Micah wanted to contribute. The first time it happened, I felt wonderful to spend money on their happiness. The second time in the same week I experienced less happiness, and did not expect him to pay. He is a VP in a high-tech company and makes lots of money.

It turns out that giving to charity may or may not increase happiness, depending on your social connection to the charity. If you click on a link to donate to an organization like Goodwill, you may not experience as much happiness as donating to a cause you are involved in. For example, I donate monthly to the Thich Nhat Hanh Foundation and it makes me happy because I am deeply involved in the Plum Village tradition. I'm not nearly as happy when I take a bundle of used clothing to Goodwill. How does this fit with your experience?

When thousands of people were asked, "What do you want in a relationship," the vast majority said they want kindness – loving kindness. Our practice is to establish ourselves and sources of loving kindness. To do this, it is most important to begin with ourselves. We can shower loving kindness blessings on ourselves and actually come to experience more loving kindness for ourselves. This will flow out to others, as Ruth King said, "Loving kindness is a genuine desire for all beings, without exception, to be safe from inner and outer harm, to be healthy and content, and to live with ease." John Kabat-Zinn, founder of Mindfulness Based Stress Reduction (MBSR) said,

> *Once you have established yourself as a center of love and kindness radiating throughout your being, which amounts to a cradling of yourself in loving kindness and acceptance, you can dwell here indefinitely, drinking at this fount, bathing in it, renewing yourself, nourishing yourself, enlivening yourself. This can be a profoundly healing practice for body and soul.*

The Buddha's teachings on loving kindness are in a document called the *metta sutra* which asks us to spread loving kindness over the entire world – to everyone, with unconditional love. Here is how it goes:

> Let none deceive another,
> Or despise any being in any state.
> Let none through anger or ill-will
> Wish harm upon another.
> Even as a mother protects with her life
> Her child, her only child,
> So with a boundless heart
> Should one cherish all living beings;
> Radiating kindness over the entire world:
> Spreading upwards to the skies,
> And downwards to the depths;
> Outwards and unbounded,
> Freed from hatred and ill-will.
> Whether standing or walking, seated or lying down
> Free from drowsiness,
> One should sustain this recollection.
> This is said to be the sublime abiding.
> By not holding to fixed views,
> The pure-hearted one, having clarity of vision,
> Being freed from all sense desires,
> Is not born again into this world.
> ~The Metta Sutra

Kevin Griffin, an insight meditation teacher, put it this way:

> Unconditional Love
> The Metta Sutta tells us to spread love over the entire world to everyone, no matter what we think or feel about them. This is unconditional love, love that doesn't expect or need a return, love that sees past the petty differences and disputes in life to the universal longings for happiness that we all share.

Jack Kornfield in my teacher training program told this story about Sharon Salzberg, two of the three people to bring Insight

Meditation to the North America in the 1970's:

> Sharon Salzberg, again, in this book Real Love, tells a story when she was first practicing metta [loving kindness] as in intensive practice, going, OK, may I be peaceful, may I be happy, may I be filled with love, her metta phrases, on and on. She said, "It felt very mechanical and nothing was happening." And she was doing it over and over. And then she was on her way to go downstairs, maybe to meet with the teacher. And she dropped the tray that she was carrying with these things on it, and glass shattered on the floor and all this stuff. And she said to herself, "Sharon, you're such a klutz," which is what she usually said in her mind. "Sharon, you're such a klutz, but I love you." And then she said, "Oh, it's working."

So I think that practice *metta* can work for us! Remember what Mark Twain said, "Kindness is the language which the deaf can hear and the blind can see." Loving kindness is the heart of love turned towards the good qualities of ourselves or others while compassion (next chapter) is the heart of love turned towards suffering. Loving kindness is the fervent desire to establish happiness and joy in all beings.

There is a story about "The Girl with the Apple," which may be an amazing true story. You can find the whole story online and here is a synopsis.

The story takes place during World War II in 1942. A Polish family was taken from their home to a concentration camp in Germany including an eleven year old boy who was tall and told to lie about his age. He said he was sixteen when he was actually eleven. He was called, "94983". This put him in circumstances where he could be put to work rather than being put to death.

A couple of days after arriving, 94983 was walking around the camp behind the barracks near the outer fence. This was a place where the guards could barely see him. He saw a girl half-hidden behind a tree. He asked her, "Do you have anything to eat?" The girl approached him and gave him an apple and told him to return the next day for another one. They couldn't talk to each other because of the danger involved.

After a while, the boy was moved to another camp with his brother and they were eventually freed in 1945. The boy would later wind up in England and still later in New York City. His friend from England tried to set him up with a blind date, and he was reluctant. Finally he gave in. The blind date was Roma, the girl with the apple all those years back at the concentration camp. They wound up getting married with two children and three grandchildren. His name was Herman Rosenblat.

Even if the story is not true, it does make for a good example of loving kindness. Can you remember a time when you acted with loving kindness? How did it happen? What did you do? Mostly, how did you feel afterwards? Try this practice every day until it becomes a habit, even if you have to recall the same action all the time. Thich Nhat Hanh wrote this about Valentine's Day:

> "Love is a living, breathing thing. There is no need to force it to grow in a particular direction. If we start by being easy and gentle with ourselves, we will find it is just there inside of us, solid and healing.
> "The first element of true love is loving kindness. The essence of loving kindness is being able to offer happiness. You can be the sunshine for another person. You can't offer happiness until you have it for yourself. So build a home inside by accepting yourself and learning to love and heal yourself. Learn how to practice mindfulness in such a way that you can create moments of happiness and joy for your own nourishment. Then you have something to offer the other person."

It is important to practice wise intention to bring more happiness into our lives and the lives of the people around us. Wise intention includes these three aspects:

1. Renunciation or letting go of unreasonable desires that take us out of the present moment
2. Loving kindness to eliminate ill will and support

happiness
3. Compassion to counter cruelty and help us wake up to realize joy

THE PRACTICE OF LOVING KINDNESS

As we develop the capacity for loving kindness, we come to realize that it does not involve positive thinking or some type of positive attitude. We don't even have to have feelings of love or kindness to practice. We just move along with the practice in such a way as to water the seeds of our positive intention. We pay attention only to wholesome intentions rather than watering the seeds of unwholesome intentions. We develop the wholesome intentions within us.

Sharon Salzberg (recalling the story, above) and Joseph Goldstein, two of the teachers who brought insight meditation to the West, wrote this about Practice Loving Kindness:

> *The practice of metta [lovingkindness] is, at a certain level, the fruition of all we work toward in our meditation. It relies on our ability to open continuously to the truth of our actual experience, not cutting off the painful parts, and not trying to pretend things are other than they are. Just as spiritual growth grinds to a halt when we indulge our tendency to grasp and cling, metta can't thrive in an environment that is bound to desire or to getting our expectations met.*

The traditional practice of loving kindness revolves around the repetition of phrases and this is not the only way to practice. We begin by offering loving kindness to ourselves. If that is not possible, we offer loving kindness towards a benefactor or someone we deeply love. Then we offer loving kindness to a benefactor or someone we deeply love or ourselves, if we chose a benefactor for our first offering. This is followed by offering loving kindness to a dear friend, a neutral person, a difficult person and finally to all beings.

> *The Buddha said that the object of our practice should be first of all, our own self. Your ability to love another person depends on your ability to love yourself. Thich Nhat Hanh says, "If you're not able to accept yourself, how could you accept another person?" In metta practice, receiving care from the benefactor or ally is so that love and caring for your own self increases. Because we are truly born for love. As you learn to receive love from others, this deepens your love for your own self. And this metta manifests in the world around you. - Pawan Bareja*

Once we select a person or group that we want to shower loving kindness blessings on, we repeat a set of three or four phrases which help us cultivate loving kindness. In our practice together, we will use the traditional set of phrases is

> *May I be safe and protected.*
> *May I be happy.*
> *May I be healthy and strong.*
> *May I live with ease.*

In my practice, I have seven sets of phrases that I use. These phrases incorporate all of the divine abodes. There are phrases for loving kindness, compassion, sympathetic joy and equanimity.

When I participated in a week long home retreat on the divine abodes in the spring of 2021 with Donald Rothberg and Kaira Jewel Lingo, Donald taught,

> *Sense the energy of the heart, the energy of metta kindness, warmth, friendliness and let it radiate out. In front, in back, left and right, above and below, the energy of kindness touching every being where you are with the wish that each might be well, might be happy the energy of metta radiating out in all six directions, filling the space around you. Let this radiating from the heart continue and expand, out to the entirety of the land. The forest, the hills, all the other beings here: the human beings, the birds, all the different*

beings. Wishing well for all the beings in the space we're radiating into, meeting all beings with this radiating kindness.

LOVING KINDNESS PRACTICE

Step 1:
We begin by taking six deep breaths. When you breathe in..., breathe in completely and deeply..., filling your chest and abdomen as fully as possible... When you breathe out..., simply let go of all the air and the tensions you are holding... [Repeat a minimum of three to six times.]
Breathe in completely and deeply... Hold your breath for a count of three... Let go and release all the air in your lungs...
Breathe in deeply again... Hold for a count of three... Let go...
Breathe in again to your full capacity... Hold for a count of three... Breathe out and release...
In... in... in... One... Two... Three... Out... out... out...
Breathe in deeply again... Hold for a count of three... Let go...
Breathe in again to your full capacity... Hold for a count of three... Breathe out and release...
Now discontinue breathing deeply... and allow your breath to naturally return to normal... Take your time... Take it easy...

Step 2:
Now that your breathing has become normal... Withdraw yourself... into yourself... Become aware of your body... Notice how your body is connected to the earth... Open your senses... Taste inside your mouth and on your lips... The smell of air coming in your nostrils... Notice the ambient sounds... Don't become attached to them... Let them go... And sight... Eyes resting... insight opening... investigation opening... imagination opening... And touch... Notice your feet and legs... Notice your hips and pelvis... Notice your abdomen and lower back... Notice your rib cage and middle back... Notice your chest and upper back... Be aware of your shoulders... On down to your arms, hands and fingers... Notice your neck and the back of your head... Notice

your face...
Continue to breathe naturally...
[Now continue being aware of your body until you are ready to move on.]
Be aware... of no other spaces... but these spaces...
Be aware... of no other times... but these times...
Be here... Be now... Be here, now...

Step 3:
When you are centered and ready, begin repeating these phrases mentally for about two minutes (or more if you wish):

> *May I be safe and protected.*
> *May I be happy.*
> *May I be healthy and strong.*
> *May I live with ease.*

[If you have difficulty with these phrases for yourself, think of a benefactor you could offer the phrases to and replace *I* with *you* instead.]

Step 4:
Repeat Step 3 for your benefactor replacing *I* with *you*, unless you began with your benefactor, in which case use the phrases as they are.

Step 5:
Now continue as is Step 4 for your dear friend, a neutral person, a difficult person and all beings. "May all beings be happy!"

    How was the practice for you? Did you have any difficulties? If so, how did you resolve them? Do you think you will continue this practice? If you do, you will find that with each repetition your loving kindness will grow immeasurably. You might want to write down some of your thoughts about this in your journal.
    For completeness, I'll end this chapter by listing the phrases that I use in my loving kindness practice, thanks to Phillip Moffitt,

founder of the Marin Sangha in which I am a member:

> *May I be safe from inner and outer harm.*
> *May I have a calm, clear mind and a peaceful, loving heart.*
> *May I be physically strong, healthy and vital.*
> *May I experience love, joy, wonder and wisdom in this life just as it is.*

I usually follow these phrases with

> *May I be peaceful and at ease.*
> *May my heart remain open.*
> *May I know the beauty and the radiance of my own Buddhanature (true nature).*
> *May I be happy, truly happy.*

Are you truly happy now? How did this practice work for you? Did you have any difficulties? Please be sure to savor this experience to create new neural pathways in your brain. You may even want to journal about your experience.

You can use any phrases you want so long as they have the sense of loving kindness in them. Also, it is best to coordinate the phrases with your breath. In the following example, I offer breath coordination hints and you can do whatever feels right to you. Plain *italics* is for the in breath and Bold ***italics*** is for the out breath. Practice in any way that is comfortable for you.

> *May I be **safe** and **protected**.*
> *May I be **happy**.*
> *May I be **healthy** and **strong**.*
> *May I live **with** ease.*

Synchronizing with your breath will help you to relax more deeply and feel the full effect of the words.

CHAPTER 6: COMPASSION

The second of the divine abodes is compassion (*karuna*). It is compassion for ourselves, known as *self-compassion* and compassion for others. Compassion is all inclusive, as Sharon Salzberg said in Seeing Our Oneness,

> *Because compassion is a state of mind that is itself open, abundant, and inclusive, it allows us to meet pain more directly. With direct seeing, we know that we are not alone in our suffering and that no one need feel alone when in pain. Seeing our oneness is the beginning of our compassion, and it allows us to reach beyond aversion and separation.*

The Dalai Lama thinks that

> *"The root of peace of mind is compassion. As soon as most of us are born our mothers take care of us and give us our first lessons in compassion. Without this we would not survive. This is how our life begins."*

It is a quivering of the heart when we recognize our own suffering and the suffering of another. Compassion is the willingness and the capacity to feel someone's suffering and to do something about it. Thay said,

> *Love is a mind that brings peace, joy, and happiness to another person. Compassion is a mind that removes the suffering that is present in the other. We all have the seeds of love and compassion in our minds, and we can develop these fine and wonderful sources of energy. We can nurture the unconditional love that does not expect anything in return and therefore does not lead to anxiety and sorrow.*

Compassion is the innate quality of the heart that wants to help and respond to someone's misfortune. It is the heart that trembles in the face of suffering. It is that quality of the heart that wants to help and respond to someone's misfortune. Wendy Hasenkamp, in *Train Your Brain* said,

> "With dedication, we can slowly build healthy mental tendencies, for awareness and wisdom, for kindness and compassion. That's why we practice."

Loving kindness and compassion go together and support each other. They are linked together so that loving kindness furthers compassion and compassion reinforces loving kindness. These are two interacting practices which when combined together help us to generate happiness and joy. This is explained very well by Karma Trinlay Rimpoche, a Tibetan teacher:

> Love and Compassion
> The two feelings of love and compassion are intimately linked. Without love, compassion cannot arise, and compassion always involves having love. Without love one would not have compassion for others' pain; instead you would probably have pity, if not total indifference. It is because of love that the suffering of other beings becomes so unbearable that a bodhisattva would endure any pain to help them.

Speaking of pity, the near neighbor of compassion is pity. Pity lacks the component of wanting to help someone who is suffering. True compassion wants to relieve the suffering of a person or other sentient being. For example, when Lego, my son's dog, had a tumor removed, he instinctively wanted to ease his own suffering by licking his wound from the surgery. With compassion, my son and Ashley, his wife, saw him doing that. They carefully placed a funnel over his head so he could no longer lick his wound. They showed all the wisdom of being compassionate toward the dog that they love.

SELF-COMPASSION

Kristin Neff at the University of Texas, Austin, is "the mistress of self-compassion." Her extensive research in compassion in general and self-compassion in particular has basically created a whole new branch of research. I took one of her two day workshops at Spirit Rock Meditation Center several years ago with my daughter, Rachael. Her kindness, openness and compassion were palpable during the whole workshop. She emphasizes that self-compassion is a practice that can prepare us for compassion for our loved ones and the world. She explains,

> The three components of self-compassion - kindness, common humanity, and mindfulness - take on a particular form when we turn toward our pain with tenderness.
> 1. Kindness manifests as love. When our hearts are open, we can warmly embrace whatever arises in our experience with gentleness and care.
> 2. Recognition of common humanity provides a sense of connection. By remembering that everyone experiences pain - that no one is perfect or leads a trouble-free life - we don't feel so alone.
> 3. Mindfulness gives us the perspective needed to present with what is, rather than contracting in fear or shame.

This can be thought of as *loving, connected presence*, and she often teaches as such. Self-kindness can be seen as treating yourself like your child or best friend with care and understanding. Common humanity is seeing oneself as part of a larger humanity. We all know the shit happens, it's impermanent, no one is exempted and that life is imperfect. It happens to all of us, Mindfulness allows us to be with the painful feelings just as they are without suppression and running away.

Self-compassion has been shown to be linked to well-being. It also curbs anxiety and reduces shame. It can help to relieve depression and stress. On the other hand, it has been shown to increase life satisfaction, happiness and self-confidence. Self-compassion provides the emotional safety needed to mindfully open to our pain and shame.

Kristin runs the Center for Mindful Self-Compassion with Chris

Germer, a professor at Harvard University. They talk about how gratitude can become a key into learning self-compassion. "True gratitude," they say, "is authentic and does not disregard the potential struggles of life." They continue,

> Let's pause on this for a moment. Think back to a time where you were having a bad day. Did you try to superficially glue gratitude onto that painful situation? If so, you likely noticed a fair amount of resistance.
> That's because gratitude is a wisdom practice. And part of practicing wisdom is understanding the complexity of your situation. So when you extend your practice to gratitude, you can acknowledge the many factors—big and small, difficult and easy, sad and joyful—that contribute to your life.

They go on to state that

> ... gratitude and savoring are important elements of a self-compassion practice. Gratitude has been shown to help people more easily notice the good within themselves and others.
> When you apply the self-compassion component of common humanity to gratitude, it helps you appreciate all the people and experiences that have helped to shape you, which may also generate a grateful feeling toward your experiences.

So the components of self-compassion are kindness towards ourselves, recognition of our common humanity and mindfulness of what is going on right now in our everyday life. This can be expressed as a connected, loving presence.

THE PRACTICE OF COMPASSION

In general, the practice of compassion proceeds in a way to the loving kindness practice we did in the last chapter using phrases which generate compassion. With the important element of self-compassion, we will deviate from the loving kindness practice to make sure we have all the bases of self-compassion included.

Remember the three components of self-compassion are kindness, common humanity and mindfulness. So the first step in practicing self-compassion is to have a kind attitude towards ourselves. Once we have this attitude, we recognize that just like us, millions of people are suffering in the same way we are.

With self-compassion, we begin to look deeply at our pain. This helps us to grow and make the changes in our lives that we deeply desire. We will wind up making much better choices for ourselves and at the same time develop more compassion for others. This may be difficult to practice, as Ofosu Jones-Quartey, a meditation teacher and musician from the Washington DC area said [emphasis mine],

> *The Need for Self-Compassion*
> **One of the hardest things for us to practice is self-compassion.** *This has been true in my own life. My loud inner critic, coupled with my mental/emotional tendency toward intrusive negative thoughts, anxiety and depression, have made self-compassion both a challenge and purpose in my life.*
> *In my time as a teacher, father, friend, etc. I've found that this is true not just for myself but for many of us. Maybe there are things we have a hard time forgiving ourselves for, maybe we were taught from our parents or friends or religious upbringings that we didn't truly matter or that it was wrong or selfish to show ourselves love. Nothing, however, could be further from the truth. Self kindness, self-compassion, are so important to this life of ours. They are Vital with a capital "V"...*

Kirstin Neff agrees with this:

> *Practicing self-compassion can be difficult and even scary. When we give ourselves love, sometimes we remember all the conditions under which we were unloved. When we open*

> to our pain, feelings we've repressed for a lifetime may rise up and overwhelm us.

Elsewhere, she gives us some hope:

> One of the most important strengths that self-compassion provides is the ability to care for others without losing ourself. Whether we're professional caregivers or caring for loved ones, stress and burnout often accompany our good work.

And,

> Self-compassion involves mindful acceptance of our pain but also care and concern for ourselves because we're hurting. We can use self-compassion to help us work with challenging feelings in five specific ways when they arise. These are combined in a practice we teach in MSC called Soften, Soothe and Allow.

COMPASSION PRACTICE

The following practice is based on an idea that I had when it was my turn to lead a meditation on one of the divine abodes to my peer group in the mindfulness teacher certification course. I had had a difficult day dealing with an internet phone problem that finally resolved itself with my technical skills. This is basically the practice I taught.

Step 1:
We begin by taking six deep breaths. When you breathe in..., breathe in completely and deeply..., filling your chest and abdomen as fully as possible... When you breathe out..., simply let go of all the air and the tensions you are holding... [Repeat a minimum of three to six times.]
  Breathe in completely and deeply... Hold your breath for a count of three... Let go and release all the air in your lungs...

Breathe in deeply again... Hold for a count of three... Let go...

Breathe in again to your full capacity... Hold for a count of three... Breathe out and release...

In... in... in... One... Two... Three... Out... out... out...

Breathe in deeply again... Hold for a count of three... Let go...

Breathe in again to your full capacity... Hold for a count of three... Breathe out and release...

Now discontinue breathing deeply... and allow your breath to naturally return to normal... Take your time... Take it easy...

Step 2:
Now that your breathing has become normal... Withdraw yourself... into yourself... Become aware of your body... Notice how your body is connected to the earth... Open your senses... Taste inside your mouth and on your lips... The smell of air coming in your nostrils... Notice the ambient sounds... Don't become attached to them... Let them go... And sight... Eyes resting... insight opening... investigation opening... imagination opening... And touch... Notice your feet and legs... Notice your hips and pelvis... Notice your abdomen and lower back... Notice your rib cage and middle back... Notice your chest and upper back... Be aware of your shoulders... On down to your arms, hands and fingers... Notice your neck and the back of your head... Notice your face...

Continue to breathe naturally...

[Now continue being aware of your body until you are ready to move on.]

Be aware... of no other spaces... but these spaces...

Be aware... of no other times... but these times...

Be here... Be now... Be here, now...

Step 3:
To cultivate compassion, please bring to mind someone who has a lot of compassion for what you are going through.... This could be a dear friend, a loved one, a child, and animal or a benefactor that is capable of offering compassion. Choose someone you deeply love.... Notice how they hold you in your heart... Sit quietly with

the feelings of compassion that you experience from this person or animal.... Now imagine this being wishing you compassion with these phrases:

> *May you take refuge in yourself*
> *May you be well*
> *May you be kind to yourself and others*
> *May you accept your life as it is*

Continue this practice for a few minutes or more.

Step 4:
Thank your loving being and allow this wishes to touch your heart... Recognize that they, too, have pain and sorrow... Then begin to offer compassion to the other being using the same phrases with kindness, tenderness and love. Continue for a few minutes or more.

Step 5:
After offering compassion to others, allow this compassion to move kindly towards yourself... Recognize that just like your being, you want happiness and avoid suffering... Just like them, offer these phrases to yourself:

> *May I take refuge in myself*
> *May you I well*
> *May I be kind to myself and others*
> *May I accept my life as it is*

Practice like this for a few minutes or more.

When you have completed the self-compassion part of the practice (Step 5), take a few minutes to contemplate your experience. What did you experience? What did you learn about compassion for yourself and others? You can even take some time to make a few notes in your journal, if you have one. Be sure to savor the experience so that new neural pathways can make their way into your brain.

CHAPTER 7: SYMPATHETIC JOY

Twenty-six years ago, when I came across the Divine Abodes, I kind of understood loving kindness because my wife has been so kind to me and other people since we met in 1974. She was always kind and considerate of my son and she took great care to make sure he was safe, comfortable and healthy.

I understood compassion to some extent because the Dalai Lama and many other teachers had talked about compassion in so many different ways. It was real to me when I was with someone who was suffering and I wanted to reach out and help somehow. This was especially true when my children were ill or when I would counsel cancer patients. I could feel and understand their pain and want to do something about it.

I understood equanimity because of some moments in my meditation practice I would feel a touch of equanimity. Also, when I did walking meditation or other practices, I could feel it. I could feel it sometimes in my work when I was in the zone and coding line after line of some computer language or other.

When it came to sympathetic joy, I was at a loss until one day in the spring of 1997, shortly after my cancer diagnosis, I was watching my daughter, Rachael, play in a tennis match. I noticed the glee and happiness she was experiencing just being out on the tennis court. I immediately got the sense of sympathetic joy – the joy that arises when you tune into the joy that someone is experiencing. Since then, I have made sympathetic joy a practice by being more aware of other peoples' happiness.

Christiane Wolf, MD and Buddhist teacher at Los Angeles Insight Meditation Center put it this way:

> *How to Practice Sympathetic Joy*
> *In the Buddha's teachings, sympathetic joy or being happy for another's happiness* [Pali: mudita] *is one of the four brahmaviharas, the four highest qualities of the heart. In recent years, the other three "loving-kindness, compassion, and equanimity" have received quite a lot of attention from practitioners, researchers, and the press alike. But sympathetic joy has gotten little attention. How can that*

be? Shouldn't joy be the most appealing of the heart qualities? Not necessarily. Traditionally it is often referred to as the most difficult of the four. Sympathetic joy is complicated.

Once you get into this practice, it will become one of your favorites. The reason is that if you practice carefully, with wise intention and savor the joy, you will create new neural pathways in your brain that will become much easier to connect to on a day to day basis. For example, when my family is together and my children, their spouses and my granddaughter are connecting to each other, that particular neural pathway of sympathetic joy gets triggered and I feel joyful. When Jessica calls me from Barcelona, I feel joyful. When I am able to greet people during walking meditation, I feel joyful. When Ada (my granddaughter) runs up to me and gives me a hug, I feel joyful. And when these events happen mostly together, I am especially grateful – grateful for my family, grateful for my practice and grateful that I have cultivated this joy to the fullest.

Sympathetic joy is my favorite of all the divine abodes. They are all wonderful and this one is special for me because it is the one that I find easiest to practice. In fact, I love all of the divine abodes, all the four immeasurable minds, the immeasurables, or whatever you want to call them. These are just wonderful teachings.

To understand sympathetic joy, we have to understand that it is the awareness of another's well being, devoid of any expectations whatsoever. We celebrate happiness. My parents used to refer to this as the *kvelling* of the heart and *nachas* - pride or gratification, especially at the achievements of one's children. You may recall from the early chapter how much *nachas* I have for my three children, their spouses and my granddaughter.

You might want to begin thinking about a time when you felt this kind of feeling of real joy in somebody else's happiness. It's a wonderful feeling – one of those forces of joy and happiness that modern science hasn't gotten to yet (as far as I know). Thich Nhat Hanh says,

> *"Sympathetic joy arises when one rejoices over the happiness of others and wishes others well-being and success."*

As much difficulty as I had in understanding this, you may not have the same difficulty because you may have already recognized something that gave you joy in somebody else's success. I thought it was the most difficult one and you may not find it so.

Sympathetic joy is a natural expression of our best humanity and I think that it is something that is totally lacking in our society today – being natural and being friendly and wishing the best for everybody. This whole competitive milieu is really destroying us, especially the people who are fighting in Ukraine. So it becomes very important to celebrate buoyancy and health and happiness whenever it is encountered. We need to celebrate all that is good in the world.

Sympathetic joy is related to loving kindness through the idea that when loving kindness encounters the good fortunes of others it transforms into appreciative joy. Andrew Olendzki, a Buddhist teacher and scholar writes,

> *When lovingkindness encounters the good fortune and happiness of another, it transforms into appreciative joy. This is the emotion of feeling good for another person, of being glad that good things are happening for them. Appreciative joy arises easily for the people we care about, but so often its opposite "some form of jealousy, envy, or resentment" comes up for us. The antidote for these forms of discontent is learning how to feel good for others, which generally takes a lot of practice.*

And there is an almost instant connection to gratitude, for the joy in another and for our own experience.

When we feel sympathetic joy, we cannot also have the feeling of jealousy or envy. Sympathetic joy is the opposite of jealousy and it is impossible to hold the two at the same time. Jorge Ferrer, a US-based Spanish psychologist, wrote about this:

> Transforming Jealousy into Joy
> The transformation of jealousy through the cultivation of sympathetic joy [the capacity to participate in the joy of others] bolsters the awakening of the enlightened heart.

Sympathetic joy, along with loving kindness and compassion has the quality of looking at the good things in life. Thinking about the good things helps us to be happy and maintain a positive attitude towards our lives. Tempel Smith, a teacher at the Spirit Rock Meditation Center in Woodacre, California says (emphasis mine),

> One thing you'll notice about compassion, lovingkindness, and sympathetic joy is that they have a **preference for what's good**, and an understanding that pain and suffering is a misfortune we all face. And yet that preference for the good, and seeing what's painful as a misfortune, will keep us in our reactivity. With deeper wisdom, as we become intimate with life, as we have lived long enough and felt into what an actual human life is like, we see that there is this up and down motion: there's pleasure and good fortune, then states that are very difficult when we experience pain and loss. To be an open-hearted human means that we have to come to terms with the fact that there will be some pleasure, there will be some pain, and that we don't have much control over that. And so equanimity grows over time, with perspective.

Yes, we will all have times of trouble, pain and suffering. This is the nature of all existence. Even the trees and plants have difficulties. Our pets suffer in much the same way that we do. However, if we cultivate states of happiness and joy, we can use this as medicine for our hearts. Andrew Olendzki wrote,

> The next time you experience discontent, deliberately

> cultivate appreciative joy "gladness at the good fortune of others" as an antidote. Everything need not always be about us. Other people deserve to feel happy and have good fortune, and even if we ourselves are in the doldrums for some reason we can vicariously experience the well-being of others. Appreciative joy is always accessible; we merely need to reach for it.

We can learn to understand how joy can manifest when we are down in the dumps by thinking about the joy of others. Andrew says,

> Learn to discern the different ways joy can manifest in your experience. In particular, see if you can get a good felt sense of what the special quality of appreciative joy feels like. This is the emotion of feeling good about good things happening to other people. Practice calling to mind the goodness of others, and then settle into the emotion of wishing them well and appreciating their success in a way that is not about you.

When we savor an experience of sympathetic joy, we create neural pathways in our brain which provide a kind of positive feedback loop to produce more sympathetic joy. This has the effect of increasing our happiness and joy in every increasing way. We begin to find joy in walking in nature or seeing a beautiful sunset or having a loving conversation with our beloved. Our minds get more used to experiences and drift away from wanting things. I know this for myself and I wish I had listened to my teachers in the 1970's, especially Father Eli and Rajneesh. The research supports this, as Oren Jay Sofer, a Buddhist teach, said,

> There are four distinct circuits in the brain that are essential for well-being in humans: the ability to maintain positive states, the ability to recover from negative states of mind--those are two distinct skills--the ability to focus the mind, and the ability to be generous. Studies show that the

more our mind wanders, the less happy we are. And we tend to wander into states of discontent more than states of bliss or happiness. The practice of appreciative joy crosses into each of these. It's interesting to see that there's an entire kind of circuit in the mind devoted to giving--to the joy we feel at cooperating and collaborating as humans.

I want to close this section with a quote from the Buddha, himself:

> Whatever you intend, whatever you plan, and whatever you have a tendency toward, that will become the basis upon which your mind is established. (SN 12.40) Develop meditation on appreciative joy, for when you develop meditation on appreciative joy, any discontent will be abandoned. (MN 62)
> Suppose there were a pond with lovely smooth banks, filled with pure water that was clear and cool. A person scorched and exhausted by hot weather, weary, parched, and thirsty, would come upon the pond and quench their thirst and their hot-weather fever. In just the same way a person encounters the teachings of the Buddha and develops appreciative joy, and thereby gains internal peace. (MN 40)

Note: *SN* refers to Samyutta Nikaya, one of the collections of Buddha's teachings. *MN* refers to the middle discourses of the Buddha. These were left in the quote for completeness.

THE PRACTICE OF SYMPATHETIC JOY

Sympathetic joy doesn't really need a lot of practice once you have experienced it. For example, when I offered a practice of sympathetic joy to my students in the practicum, I kept it as short as possible. At the end of the practice, I asked the students about their experience. As each person shared their experience, the other students were feeling joy for the person sharing. As time went on, the joy and love in the Zoom room increased. I felt certain that everybody in the class understood and bodily felt sympathetic joy.

SYMPATHETIC JOY PRACTICE

Step 1:
We begin by taking six deep breaths. When you breathe in..., breathe in completely and deeply..., filling your chest and abdomen as fully as possible... When you breathe out..., simply let go of all the air and the tensions you are holding... [Repeat a minimum of three to six times.]
Breathe in completely and deeply... Hold your breath for a count of three... Let go and release all the air in your lungs...
Breathe in deeply again... Hold for a count of three... Let go...
Breathe in again to your full capacity... Hold for a count of three... Breathe out and release...
In... in... in... One... Two... Three... Out... out... out...
Breathe in deeply again... Hold for a count of three... Let go...
Breathe in again to your full capacity... Hold for a count of three... Breathe out and release...
Now discontinue breathing deeply... and allow your breath to naturally return to normal... Take your time... Take it easy...

Step 2:
Now that your breathing has become normal... Withdraw yourself... into yourself... Become aware of your body... Notice how your body is connected to the earth... Open your senses... Taste inside your mouth and on your lips... The smell of air coming in your nostrils... Notice the ambient sounds... Don't become attached to them... Let them go... And sight... Eyes resting... insight opening... investigation opening... imagination opening... And touch... Notice your feet and legs... Notice your hips and pelvis... Notice your abdomen and lower back... Notice your rib cage and middle back... Notice your chest and upper back... Be aware of your shoulders... On down to your arms, hands and fingers... Notice your neck and the back of your head... Notice your face...
Continue to breathe naturally...
[Now continue being aware of your body until you are ready to

move on.]
Be aware... of no other spaces... but these spaces...
Be aware... of no other times... but these times...
Be here... Be now... Be here, now...

Step 3:
Now I invite you to look around you with your mind to find good things happening to other people. This could be from today or last week or month... I'm sure you can find something that is wholesome and has a good feeling about it... It can seem hard to find because of the negative bias of our new sources. If you search a little, you can find some good news somewhere... When you do, allow yourself to be glad and joyful for those people or that person. Share in their appreciation and gratitude...

You can only feel sympathetic joy when you see or think about the success of others. So look for it... You may find it in the smile of a young child... You may find it when you are watching a movie where somebody has good things happening for them... If you are fortunate, you may notice it every day. You hear some good news about a person overcoming a disastrous illness... You may learn of a couple celebrating a happy marriage, whether for the first time or the nth time...

I often think about the happiness that my children experience in their lives... That is a wonderful thing because you don't need to be out anywhere. You can do it in the silence of your own home...

Notice these moments when you feel sympathetic joy for someone because it has a strong effect on your own happiness... Now if many instances come to mind, please choose just one right now for this practice... Think about what their success was or their happiness was. Think about what changed in their lives. Think about how love was manifested in that experience with them... You might ask, "What is love asking of me today?"

As this meditation comes to an end, please keep these thoughts and feelings in mind.

Now please take a few moments to savor your experience of

sympathetic joy. You may even want to write down what you experienced. If you had been in my class, I would have liked you to share your experience with the group. If you wish, you can send me an email with your experience: jerome [@] mountainsangha [dot] org.

Note: the third step, above is a transcription of what I taught in April of 2022 to my class. You will find the recording on the resources page on my website: mountainsangha.org/resources-for-the-divine-abodes.

Also, there are phrases you can use if you prefer to follow the examples in loving kindness and compassion. Here is a set that I have used:

May your happiness and good fortune continue
May they increase
May they never wane

CHAPTER 8: EQUANIMITY

We now have come to the last chapter and the last of the divine abodes: equanimity. Thich Nhat Hanh calls this limitless quality, inclusiveness. Other teachers use the term, detachment. So let's see if we can break down these different terms. Equanimity means an evenly balanced mind. It also connotes even-mindedness, non-reactivity, non-preferential, tolerance, forbearance, and inclusiveness.

My friend and beloved teacher, - Kaira Jewel Lingo, former nun with Thich Nhat Hanh uses equanimity and inclusiveness interchangeably:

> THE IMMEASURABLE PEACE OF EQUANIMITY
> "The practice of equanimity, of inclusiveness, can give us great courage. The Buddha said that when you have equanimity, you have a mind of immeasurable peace. When you have peace, you have a lot of freedom. And when you have freedom, you're not so afraid."

So basically, in my opinion, equanimity includes inclusiveness and to some extent it goes beyond it. For instance, Andrew Olendzki says that every moment of mindfulness is a moment of equanimity and

> Equanimity manifests as the absence of the two extremes of attraction (greed) and aversion (hatred), which so often rule the mind. Equanimity is the still center point on a continuum between the two, where the mind neither draws toward nor tilts away from an object.

With this understanding, inclusiveness would consider attraction and aversion within its scope. That is, instead of being the balance between the two, as Andrew stated, attraction and aversion would be included. Shaila Catherine, an insight meditation teach, in "Equanimity in Every Bite" says

> *Equanimity has the capacity to embrace extremes without getting thrown off balance. Equanimity takes interest in whatever is occurring simply because it is occurring. Equanimity does not include indifference, boredom, coldness, or hesitation. It is an expression of calm, radiant balance that takes whatever comes in stride.*

Equanimity is highly valued within the Buddha's teachings. When highly developed, it is the precursor to the experience of awakening. Andrew, again, clarifies detachment (emphasis mine):

> *Equanimity is the attitude and emotional state that is truly transformative. Being able to be entirely neutral while at the same time being fully aware is a special state of mind to be cherished. Neutral is sometimes regarded as a negative word, suggesting disinterest or* **detachment***, but that is not at all how it is used in the Buddhist tradition. Rather it is the pinnacle of the developed mind, the state to which the jhāna practice delivers us.*

He also said,

> *Equanimity is often confounded with indifference or detachment, but this is far from accurate. These two are mild forms of aversion in which a person chooses to push their interest away from an object or deliberately remove awareness from attending to what is present. Equanimity is the opposite of these, engaging the object with heightened awareness but without being pulled by attraction or pushed away by aversion.*

So all of this should clarify why I think we should stick with equanimity rather than inclusiveness or detachment.

Equanimity also has the property of not being tossed by the eight worldly winds: praise and blame, gain and loss, pleasure and pain, fame and disrepute. It is not caught between many other pairs of opposites and these are the ones mentioned in Buddhist literature. When you're not caught in these pairs of opposites, you rest in calm abiding and equanimity,

What really helps equanimity is forgiveness – forgiveness of yourself and forgiveness of others for not being perfect. Forgiveness has been covered in detail in chapter 5.

What is equanimity? How can we cultivate it in our mindfulness meditation practice? How can we access it in our daily lives, especially in times like these with so much uncertainty and sadness over the suffering in the world? Here is what I wrote about five years ago:

> *Gratitude*
> *Of all the teachings of Father Eli and Zen Master Thich Nhat Hanh I think that the teachings on gratitude had the most significant effect on my life. Ever since I started practicing gratitude, my life has become better and happier. I began to have a feeling of inner peace and equanimity. Appreciating what I have has given me the freedom from desiring possessions which only take up space and cost money.*

So who is the fellow, Father Eli and what does he have to do with equanimity? In 1973, I was living in Evanston, Illinois. My wife and son had moved to California. I went to a spiritual book store on Howard Avenue expecting a class on yoga. It was a rainy night and parking was difficult. When I walked into the classroom, I noticed the pudgy old man, probably in his sixties at the head of the room offering a teaching. He had a southern drawl and his voice was quite enchanting. He was giving a lecture on some of the lost wisdom teachings of the forest dwellers in Europe. I was entranced and returned the next month and the next.

He taught a guided imagery practice that had one cardinal rule: do not be attached to the outcome. I used these practices to get a job in California, to help my son recover from cancer, to help myself to recover from cancer and in many, many other ways. Each time I practiced it, I remembered that it was really important to not be attached to the results. If you are attached to the results, you have a certain amount of tension in your guided meditation that prevents things from happening. So I highly recommend this technique and I have taught it to hundreds of people, usually in one-on-one sessions over the past fifty years.

I learned later in life – sometime in the 1980s or 1990s that Father Eli had studied with and was trained by D. T. Suzuki in Japan after World War II. D. T. Suzuki was the author of a seminal book on Zen, *Manual of Zen Buddhism*, which I read in the early 1980s.

So, with equanimity, one is able to experience both pleasure and pain "without clinging to anything in the world." Here's a quote from Matthieu Ricard, a wonderful Tibetan Buddhist, a PhD biochemist, translator for the Dalai Lama and founder of Karuna-Shechen, a charitable organization dedicated to educating children in Nepal and other impoverished areas, and author of *Happiness and Altruism*:

> *Like a Mountain*
> *The practitioner's mind is likened to a mountain that the winds can't shake; he's neither tormented by the difficulties he may come across nor elated by his successes. But that equanimity is neither apathy nor indifference. It's accompanied by inner jubilation, and by an openness of mind expressed as unfailing altruism.*

THE PRACTICE OF EQUANIMITY

Equanimity can be practiced in so many ways including with phrases. For example: The traditional way is to use phrases similar to loving kindness and compassion phrases. Some phrases you might use are:

> May I open to this moment just as it is
> Things are just as they are right now
> May my heart be at ease with the conditions in my life
> All beings meet their joys and sorrows according to their

> own actions
> As much as I would like things to be different, things are just as they are in this moment

Another example: Ask the question: "What's difficult for me to accept?" After identifying what's difficult, then bring mindfulness and inquiry to the area that has surfaced. You might explore reactivity and unacknowledged pain related to particular states of affairs, assumptions and expectations about what should have happened, etc. Such inquiry can help equanimity to arise.

We are going to use a different approach in the practice of equanimity. The practice is called RAINS. RAIN is a practice originally taught by Michele McDonald and championed by Tara Brach in her book, *Radical Compassion*. RAIN is an anachronism for the following:

R – Recognize what is happening
A – Allow the experience to be just as it is
I – Investigate with interest and care
N – Nourish with self-compassion

By all means, if something is bothering you, this is a wonderful practice to help relieve your suffering. I have done it many times alone and with a partner. We are going to use the letters as follows:

R- Recall or remember or image a time of peace, balance, even-mindedness, equanimity
A - Allow the scene to fill you with great peace, balance or happiness
I - Investigate or image the causes and conditions that brought this scene alive
N - Nurture the experience
S - Savor this experience so that you can feel it again

Ready? Let's begin!

EQUANIMITY PRACTICE

Step 1:
We begin by taking six deep breaths. When you breathe in..., breathe in completely and deeply..., filling your chest and abdomen as fully as possible... When you breathe out..., simply let go of all the air and the tensions you are holding... [Repeat a minimum of three to six times.]
Breathe in completely and deeply... Hold your breath for a count of three... Let go and release all the air in your lungs...
Breathe in deeply again... Hold for a count of three... Let go...
Breathe in again to your full capacity... Hold for a count of three... Breathe out and release...
In... in... in... One... Two... Three... Out... out... out...
Breathe in deeply again... Hold for a count of three... Let go...
Breathe in again to your full capacity... Hold for a count of three... Breathe out and release...
Now discontinue breathing deeply... and allow your breath to naturally return to normal... Take your time... Take it easy...

Step 2:
Now that your breathing has become normal... Withdraw yourself... into yourself... Become aware of your body... Notice how your body is connected to the earth... Youi might say to this body, "Be safe and secure, strong and healthy..." Notice there is a heart – a heart that beats... A heart that loves... A heart that feels joy and equanimity... You might say to this heart, "Be peaceful and at ease..." Notice you have a mind, a brain, a head... You might want to say to this head, "Be there for whatever happens..." Be present...
Be aware... of no other spaces... but these spaces...
Be aware... of no other times... but these times...
Be here... Be now... Be here, now...

Step 3: Recall
Now recall or remember or imagine a time of peace in your life... A time of balance... A time when you were even mindedness... If you are able to recall more than one event of this nature, please

just choose one... If you can't choose one, try to imagine a time of peace... a time of balance... a time of mindfulness...

Step 4: Allow
Now allow this scene to fill you with great peace... with balance... with even mindedness right now in the present moment... Just allow it to be there in you... Even if you are imagining it, allow it to just be there...

Step 5: Investigate
Now let's investigate or imagine the causes and conditions that brought this scene alive... What was it about the experience that captured your attention? ... What did you see? ... Hear? ... Smell,,,? Mostly what did you feel? ... Where were you when this happened? ... Who was there with you? ... What happened that made it so alive in you right now? ... How does it feel in your body to renew the feelings of this experience? ...

Step 6: Nurture
Now take this experience as a whole and allow it to nurture you to help you find peace... to help you find even mindedness... to help you find balance... Ask yourself, "What do you need to do to allow these feelings to arise again? ,,, What is it like being with these feelings of peace... of balance... of even mindedness... of equanimity?...

Thich Nhat Hanh would say, "When the wholesome seeds of peace and equanimity come into mind consciousness, cultivate and nurture these seeds with kindness and allow it to remain." ...

The Buddha would say, "When the awakening factor of equanimity is present, be aware." ... Just be aware...

Nurture these seeds of peace, ... balance, ... equanimity with kindness and compassion... Notice that you were able to be present with the way that things were...

Step 7: Savor
Not take a moment to savor this experience so that you can find it and be with it again... Pay attention to the peace and joy that you

have... Learn to focus on the positive daily experiences...

How was this experience for you? Did you get a taste of peace and equanimity? Did you have any problems with the meditation practice? I suggest you write something down about the experience so you can refer to it at a time when you feel a little dysregulated.

CHAPTER 9: GRATITUDE AND GENEROSITY

In my own personal experience, gratitude practices have changed my life for the better and in the direction of much happiness. I have learned to think of a minimum of three people, experiences, events and / or things that I am grateful for just before I fall asleep. I have been doing this regularly since about 2015 and wish I had begun many years before. It is a simple practice and it brings to life the wonderful experiences of the day that I want to remember.

If I had listened to my root teachers, Father Eli, in the 1970s, I would have been much better off. He taught about gratitude as a spiritual practice. He taught that success in life is being grateful for what you have. He said that our gratitudes should be written down and memorized. He wrote,

We all have a list of things for which we are grateful in our lives. There is no one who doesn't have a number of these blessings even though you may also have afflictions. These afflictions may be for the purpose of teaching you a lesson. Be grateful that you have them or else you would not learn the lesson you are learning right now.

This rings true for me with regard to living with muscle invasive bladder cancer since the beginning of 1997. Once I began to understand that the cancer would be with me for a while, I settled into a friendship with it. This may have been one of the reasons that I still have my bladder when the gold standard of treatment is to remove the bladder in a surgical procedure called radical cystectomy. Working with Father Eli's teaching during my periods of recovery really helped me stay present for whatever was happening in my medical treatment and recovery.

Father Eli also wrote,

There is always something for which to be grateful for. The most important thing you have to be grateful for is the chance you have been given to work toward your own perfection in this lifetime. Make a list of the things you are grateful for and make them a part

of your daily practice .... When we tell someone we are grateful for the things given us, that person tends to give us greater and greater things.

My wife used to put it to our children this way, "To desire what you don't have is to waste what you do have." Their desires were for more toys, more clothes and more sweets. These can develop into cravings and causes for great suffering. When you waste what you do have, you are like a spoiled child who receives a gift and throws it on the ground. This is another type of poison – the poison of aversion. Craving can be countered by generosity and aversion can be calmed by kindness and gratitude.

So what is gratitude and how do we cultivate it? Gratitude is the quality of being thankful and a tendency to show appreciation for what one has or what someone has done for us. Aside from being grateful for what we have and what other people have done for us, we can express our gratitude by writing a letter of gratitude to someone who has recently helped us or who has been especially kind to us and deliver the letter in person. This is the experience of sharing gratitude with other people.

I have discovered that being grateful for what Mala does for me kind of removes the negative effects of having to do things her way. We both have learned to be grateful to each other and the happy family we have been fortunate to be part of.

The Buddha taught that we should think of the good things that our parents, teachers, friends and others have done for us and to express gratitude for them. Ajahn Sumedho, a dedicated monk in the Thai Forest Tradition writes in *How to Receive*:

The Buddha encouraged us to think of the good things done for us by our parents, by our teachers, friends, whomever; and to do this intentionally, to cultivate it, rather than just letting it happen accidentally.

This really points to being grateful for what we have received in our entire life. Along the same lines, Dr. Roger Walsh in *Essential Spirituality: The Seven Central Practices to Awaken Heart and*

Mind writes (emphasis mine on gratitude and generosity),

WHAT MAKES FOR LASTING HAPPINESS?

"Everyone wants to be happy but what makes for lasting happiness? Interestingly, research is now validating ancient wisdom in many ways. Money, for example, is surprisingly ineffective-- it can alleviate the suffering of deprivation, but above a certain minimum does precious little to increase lasting happiness.
So what does work? Many things will bump up happiness temporarily, but long term is a very different matter. Researchers have found three things that succeed in doing this. What are they?
*1) Cultivating **gratitude**, and particularly effective is writing down something each day for which you feel grateful.*
2) Reframing difficult experiences in a positive way. This, of course, is the old practice of looking for the silver lining.
*3) **Generosity**. The old wisdom is true--in giving to others we give to ourselves, and the happy result is what's called a "helper's high."*
May you be happy!"

Gratitude also promotes a strong sense of resilience – the ability to bounce back from difficult situations. I experienced this as a fact in my recovery from cancer. I bounced back from a very serious form of cancer and live to tell about it. Jack Kornfield teaches,

Gratitude, wherever we are, it becomes a way of touching the heart, of opening ourselves to something greater, to connecting with one another and to connecting with something that's magnificent. And the neuroscience of it shows that living with gratitude brings better health. You become more socially connected, more resilient, less anxious.

Tara Brach, a Buddhist teacher, founder of Insight Meditation Center of Washington (DC) and one of the teachers in my MMTCP program identifies four components of gratitude:
  1. Remembering the good.
  2. Feeling gratitude and staying with it when you do.

3. Say it out loud when you are grateful.
4. Bringing a kind presence to whatever you are feeling and the more you are with it, the more you will begin to feel appreciation for it.

The practice of gratitude is a wisdom practice. Part of the practice is the wisdom of understanding the complexity of our lives. When you practice gratitude, you can acknowledge this complexity and how it affects our life. Things can be big or small, difficult or easy, sad or joyful and we can express our gratitude for all of these situations. Thay says, "Keeping your body healthy is an expression of gratitude to the whole cosmos - the trees, the clouds, everything."

In the last chapter, we mentioned savoring as a means for reducing our tendency for hedonic adaptation. In conjunction with gratitude and generosity there are many opportunities to take a step back from our experience, review it in our minds and feelings with a lot of appreciation. Savoring is the art of stepping out of our experience to appreciate it in a way that makes the experience last and, as a result, it becomes more memorable. We can recognize savoring by our true presence for what is happening to us and enjoy it in a special way.

A good way to practice savoring is what is called the "Ten Breath Practice," devised by dharma teacher Glen Schneider. There is, in fact, a small book about it available from Parallax Press. This practice is so good for nourishing our happiness and joy and savoring a special moment. When we find ourselves in a wonderful moment of a special sight, sound, taste, smell or physical sensation (feeling), this is the time to savor it. We stop for a moment, take a brief pause, relax and open to the experience we are having with our full presence. We breathe in and out ten times keeping our minds on the experience we are having. According to Glen, this is ample time for us to create a new neural pathway in our brains. He also explains,

This practice is based in recent neuroscience, where three important discoveries have been made about nourishing happiness and joy:

1. Our brain is organized in clusters of neurons known as "neural pathways." Mental traffic tends to follow existing, readily available routes, regardless of whether the neural pathway is appropriate, accurate, or actually beneficial. The more we use a route, the more available it becomes. "What fires together, wires together."
2. The human organism is preferentially wired, overwhelmingly, to recognize dangers and threats. Survival is the priority. Happiness and joy are optional behaviors.
3. Neuroscientists have estimated that it takes about thirty seconds to firmly root a new neural pathway. So with awareness and practice, we can develop our beneficial pathways. New neural networks become more firmly rooted with the length of time something is held in awareness and with the intensity of the emotional stimulation. As new connections are created and used repeatedly, footpaths eventually become freeways. With practice we can re-wire our brains so that patterns of happiness become habitual, authentic, and deeply nourishing.

Savoring has the effect of causing us to notice that this is a wonderful moment. For example, my daughter Jessica was visiting us last August around her birthday with her husband and two friends. We invited the rest of the family including my granddaughter to join us for dinner. I experienced a wonderful moment when I recognized that every one of us was very happy together. I felt a long moment of bliss bubbling up in my body, heart and mind and I have savored this moment forever. You can believe that this was re-experienced at night when I did my gratitude practice.

This experience points out how beneficial it is to replay happy memories in our minds. As I was telling it, the feelings I had at the time came back and changed my mood for the rest of the day. It's as if I was rewinding a videotape of the experience and playing it back. So, perhaps set a timer on your phone for eight minutes and play back an experience that you savored. Sit there and replay it in your mind and then write down what happened. You are welcome to send it to me, which will once again enhance your experience. People who did this for three days in a row (a total of twenty-four minutes) had increases in happiness and positive emotions even four weeks later.

Certain types of activities can actually reduce the effects of savoring an experience. For example, if you focus on the future when the experience is over, it may not create the desired neural pathway. It is also harmful to remind yourself that the savor will be over soon or that it won't last forever. Thinking that it was not as good as you expected (read judging mind – chapter 1) or it will never be this good again can reduce the impact of savoring. Thinking about ways that the experience could have been better or telling ourselves that we didn't deserve the experience can also reduce the effect of savoring.

Gratitude and savoring are important elements of a self-compassion practice. With the help of these practices, we can more easily notice the good within ourselves and others.

There was a story from the time of the Buddha that moved me tremendously. I am indebted to H.E. Tulku Yeshi Rinpoche for this story.

A poor man asked the Buddha,
"Why am I so poor?"
The Buddha said, "You did not learn to give."
So the poor man said, "But, if I don't have anything to give?"
The Buddha said, "You have a few things:
The Face, which can give a smile;
The Mouth, you can praise or comfort others;
The Heart, it can open up to others;
The Eyes, they can look at the other with the eyes of compassion;
The Body, which can be used to help others."

Generosity

Generosity goes hand in hand with gratitude. Just think about it. When you are generous to someone, that person is going to feel gratitude for your generosity. So both of you are going to experience a boost in happiness. The giver and the receiver are one. The Buddha was known to have said that if you knew what I do about generosity, you would not let a single meal go by without offering some to others.

Jack Kornfield talked about three types of generosity. The first kind is tentative generosity. Questions arise like "Should I give or not? How much should I give or should I wait. Don't I really need to keep this in case I need it in the future?" Ultimately, you finally give it away and even this type of generosity is good.

The second type is "brotherly/sisterly giving." It has the sense of cooperation and sharing with one another. In this type, there is a heart opening and a feeling of joy in giving. However, the biggest boost in happiness is the third type of giving: "royal giving." You give the most beautiful or best thing you have.

I came across this diagram a couple of years ago and thought you might appreciate this giving spiral. It specifies even more types of giving.

The various labels are:
- Giving to impose (values / ideas /beliefs)
- Wastefulness (giving what is not needed / asked for)
- Self-interested giving (giving to get)
- Reactive giving (only when asked)
- Meager giving (just enough)
- Responsive giving (giving to an emerging need)
- Purposeful giving (with meaning / as mission)
- Fully engaged giving (resources and self)
- Affectionate giving (giving with familial love)
- Enduring giving (through and beyond lifespan)
- Selfless giving (giving what you need yourself)
- Ultimate giving (giving your life)

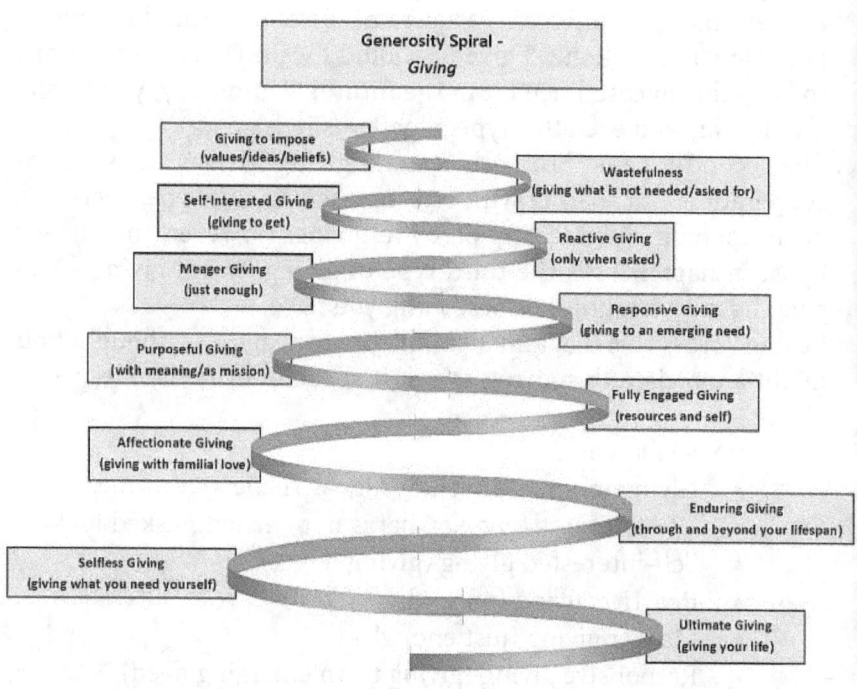

All of this points to a very important concept in Buddhist thought, that of becoming "other-oriented" and doing nice things for other people. It turns out that money spent on other people makes us happier than spending money on ourselves. This is the altruistic view that many teachers like Mathieu Ricard and the Dalai Lama consistently express. Dale Wright, an Emeritus Professor of Religious Studies at Occidental College in Los Angeles writes,

How to Become Generous
The movement from ordinary states of self-concern to selfless giving always involves a gradual transformation of character, not a sudden leap. Like any form of strength, generosity needs to be intentionally cultivated over time, and everyone must begin in whatever state of mind they already happen to be. Understanding and accepting who you really are right now is as important as the commitment to become someone more open and generous.

Whatever the quality of motivation, when we intentionally reach out to others in giving, some degree of transformation occurs. We become what we practice and do in daily life.

Forgiveness

Another practice that goes along with gratitude and generosity is forgiveness. I think it was Lily Tomlin who said, "Forgiveness means giving up all hope for a better past." Seriously, if we are unable to forgive ourselves or if we are unable to forgive others the harm that others have caused us or if we are unable to forgive the harm we have done to others, then we are holding onto much suffering. I know this from personal experience.

Around 1971, my brother, Manny, started a bakery business in Carmel Valley, California called Whole Earth Breads. The featured product was an Essene Sprouted Wheat Bread that was very popular in the health food arena. The bakery products were marketed up and down the west coast from Carmel Valley to Good Earth in Fairfax, California. That summer, I was the driver for delivering the bread to San Francisco and the North Bay. When summer ended, I had to return to Evanston, Illinois to begin teaching at Oakton Community College.

Once a month or so, Manny would call me for money. Our parents had given him some starting capital and it wasn't enough to keep the business going. So he would call me to invest more in the business. I trusted him fully.

Then things began to grow by leaps and bounds. He moved the bakery up to downtown Palo Alto and rented a place right on University Avenue. The Essene bread was extremely popular and the costs in Palo Alto skyrocketed. By 1973, I had invested about $20,000 and in 1976, I took another investment of $5,000 from a friend. Then the whole business crashed because the treasurer had neglected to pay withholding tax and the feds got wind of it. They basically shut down the business and I was out $25,000.

Over the next three decades, I kept my distance from my brother thinking that he owed me the money. When we were with our parents, I made it my business to sit on the opposite side of the table from him. I carried such resentment and suffering with me all those years. I was amazed that the harm he caused me had never crossed his mind.

This came to a head on August 5, 2011 in Central Park, New York City. Forgiveness came in a spontaneous moment when I was visiting my son and his now wife, Ashley. Micah's mother was there also. I was walking with my son, his mother Linda, and Ashley when we got the idea to honor the death of my mother by going to a Jewish deli for dinner. The previous night, we remembered Linda's father in a different Jewish deli.

I called my sister to get the exact date of my mother's passing in August of 1987. When she shocked me with the news that my brother was in the hospital in Santa Monica, California, I had to sit down to absorb her statement. Without any further thought, I prayed for my brother's rapid recovery and dropped all the resentment I had been carrying for umpteen years. I spontaneously forgave him for everything. We are talking again as he continues to recover from a serious illness, and he even came to visit me in April, 2014 and 2018. I had spent all those years suffering with resentment and loathing for him without him knowing why.

Forgiveness is the complementary practice to gratitude. This is because it is often more difficult to forgive someone than to be grateful for something someone else has done. Also, if you have not forgiven yourself or another person, you will find it difficult to shower them with loving kindness.

Often, the difficulty arises because you have not forgiven yourself for your past thoughts, words, and actions and you are holding onto them, perhaps because you feel undeserving.

But take this to heart. The act of forgiving yourself can free you from a lot of suffering. The past is already gone and you can do nothing about it. The future has not yet come so you cannot do anything about it either. We only have the present moment in which to experience the wonders of life.

They say that time heals all wounds, but the only time we have is right now. Therefore, forgiveness and the happiness that comes from it are all available in the present moment.

So part of the forgiveness practice is to first of all, forgive ourselves. I know this may sound hard to do, but with diligence and effort, it is totally possible. Another type of forgiveness is to forgive others who have harmed us. Also, we have to ask others to forgive us for whatever harm we have done to them.

Gratitude Practice
The gratitude meditation practice can be combined with the loving kindness meditation practice (next chapter) or precede or follow the mindfulness of breathing meditation practice. It can also be done alone and often during the day as things are happening in your life.
I do this practice before I go to sleep, and when I awaken. Also, many times during the day, I take note of something that I am grateful for.
The stand-alone practice begins with taking a comfortable position on a chair or cushion or lying down. If you are lying down, try not to fall asleep!

Step 1:
We begin by taking six deep breaths. When you breathe in..., breathe in completely and deeply..., filling your chest and abdomen as fully as possible... When you breathe out..., simply let go of all the air and the tensions you are holding... [Repeat a minimum of three to six times.]
Breathe in completely and deeply... Hold your breath for a count of three... Let go and release all the air in your lungs...
Breathe in deeply again... Hold for a count of three... Let go...
Breathe in again to your full capacity... Hold for a count of three... Breathe out and release...
In... in... in... One... Two... Three... Out... out... out...
Breathe in deeply again... Hold for a count of three... Let go...
Breathe in again to your full capacity... Hold for a count of three... Breathe out and release...
Now discontinue breathing deeply... and allow your breath to naturally return to normal... Take your time... Take it easy...

Step 2:
Now that your breathing has become normal... Withdraw

yourself... into yourself... Become aware of your body... Notice how your body is connected to the earth... Open your senses... Taste inside your mouth and on your lips... The smell of air coming in your nostrils... Notice the ambient sounds... Don't become attached to them... Let them go... And sight... Eyes resting... insight opening... investigation opening... imagination opening... And touch... Notice your feet and legs... Notice your hips and pelvis... Notice your abdomen and lower back... Notice your rib cage and middle back... Notice your chest and upper back... Be aware of your shoulders... On down to your arms, hands and fingers... Notice your neck and the back of your head... Notice your face...

Continue to breathe naturally...

[Now continue being aware of your body until you are ready to move on.]

Be aware... of no other spaces... but these spaces...
Be aware... of no other times... but these times...
Be here... Be now... Be here, now...

Step 3:
Bring to mind an event, object, or experience that happened today that you are truly grateful for. If you can't think of one, look back in your life and find something that you are truly grateful for.

It may be something as simple as a smile you received from someone while you were walking to or from work or the friendliness of a clerk that checked out your groceries, like in the story of the poor man. If you take notice of these kinds of acts of kindness, you will soon find yourself "paying it forward."

Now acknowledge your gratitude and feel the joy you had when the event, object, or experience took place.

Step 4:
Repeat the above at least two more or as many times as you want. Do this every day for maximum benefit. Please keep track of your gratitude practice so that you can know how much it is benefiting you.

Forgiveness Practice

The forgiveness meditation practice has three components. The first component is to ask for forgiveness from people we may have harmed. The second component is to forgive ourselves. The third component is to forgive others.

It is important to note that if we are not comfortable with any of the components or all of them, we do not have to force ourselves to do the practice. For example, if we feel we cannot forgive ourselves, we can sit quietly and look deeply to see if there is a tiny element of forgiveness that we can muster for something we did in our lives. We can look for a tiny spark that can open our hearts for forgiveness.

Similarly, if we find that we cannot forgive a certain other person, because what they "did to us" was so unforgivable, we can sit quietly and look for a tiny opening in our heart to that person. Maybe we can find a small morsel of forgiveness and forgive them for part of their actions.

Maybe, with practice, these tiny sparks and these tiny openings can blossom into a full-fledged heart opening and we can truly begin to forgive. Perhaps, there is a small offense that you no longer wish to hold onto and can use that as a lever to pry open your heart.

These small little openings can lead to full-on forgiveness if we are diligent and practice with enough patience to allow them to flower.

This practice again begins with taking a comfortable position on a chair or cushion or lying down. If you are lying down, try not to fall asleep! If you are uncomfortable with one of the components of forgiveness, skip it until you are ready to deal with it. For example, if there is someone you cannot possibly forgive right now, use another person or situation. If you can't think of anyone to forgive, begin by forgiving yourself.

Step 1:
We begin by taking six deep breaths. When you breathe in..., breathe in completely and deeply..., filling your chest and abdomen as fully as possible... When you breathe out..., simply let go of all the air and the tensions you are holding... [Repeat a

minimum of three to six times.]
Breathe in completely and deeply... Hold your breath for a count of three... Let go and release all the air in your lungs...
Breathe in deeply again... Hold for a count of three... Let go...
Breathe in again to your full capacity... Hold for a count of three... Breathe out and release...
In... in... in... One... Two... Three... Out... out... out...
Breathe in deeply again... Hold for a count of three... Let go...
Breathe in again to your full capacity... Hold for a count of three... Breathe out and release...
Now discontinue breathing deeply... and allow your breath to naturally return to normal... Take your time... Take it easy...

Step 2:
Now that your breathing has become normal... Withdraw yourself... into yourself... Become aware of your body... Notice how your body is connected to the earth... Open your senses... Taste inside your mouth and on your lips... The smell of air coming in your nostrils... Notice the ambient sounds... Don't become attached to them... Let them go... And sight... Eyes resting... insight opening... investigation opening... imagination opening... And touch... Notice your feet and legs... Notice your hips and pelvis... Notice your abdomen and lower back... Notice your rib cage and middle back... Notice your chest and upper back... Be aware of your shoulders... On down to your arms, hands and fingers... Notice your neck and the back of your head... Notice your face...
Continue to breathe naturally...
[Now continue being aware of your body until you are ready to move on.]
Be aware... of no other spaces... but these spaces...
Be aware... of no other times... but these times...
Be here... Be now... Be here, now...

Step 3:
As your breathing becomes normal, begin to feel what it feels like to have your heart closed to forgiving yourself or others. Now, as

you are sitting or lying there feeling all of this emotion, recall a time when you felt that you had harmed someone in ways that were hurtful and not necessarily intentional.

As you recall this time, allow yourself to visualize the way you hurt that person. Feel the pain that you inflicted due to your own confusion and suffering.

Now simply ask for forgiveness by saying to that person, "Please forgive me. Please release me. I'm sorry that I caused you pain."

Alternatively, you can use these more elaborate phrases for asking for forgiveness from others:

There are many ways I have harmed you, knowingly and unknowingly – betrayed you, abandoned you, caused you pain so many times. I remember these now and feel the sorrows I still carry. In the many ways I have hurt or harmed you, betrayed you, caused you suffering, out of my own fear and confusion, out of my own pain, anger and hurt and misunderstanding, in this moment, I ask your forgiveness. I ask for your forgiveness. Please forgive me. Please forgive me. May I be forgiven.[1]

If the situation that you are recalling is too difficult for you to confront at this time, be sure to forgive yourself for not being able to let it go right now. You can also choose someone that is much easier to forgive and then build up to forgiving the difficult person.

Step 4:

Take another deep breath or two to give yourself the time to release whatever charge is left over from Step 3. Then recall a time when you have hurt yourself or did something to yourself that you feel sorry for.

When you have recalled such a time, think to yourself, "I have caused myself pain and suffering for this and other thoughts, words, or actions. I now forgive myself." You may wish to repeat

---

[1] These verses were from a video on YouTube featuring Jack Kornfield.

this several times, either by recalling other events or staying with the time that you recalled.

If this step seems too difficult, tune into your feelings and try to discover what is going on. Forgive yourself for a small thing to get started, and progress gently and compassionately to what you once thought to be unforgivable.

Step 5:
Again, take one or more deep breaths to relieve yourself of the feelings and sensation that arose when you were forgiving yourself. Then, recall a time when another person caused you to suffer, either by words or actions.

Try to make this recollection as vivid as possible and bring to mind the feelings you have about it. Then remember that the person who you recalled was also suffering knowingly or unknowingly when she or he caused you harm.

Now pick a small part of this pain and say to the person, "I forgive you. I release you." Repeat this as many times as needed.

Each time you return to this forgiveness meditation, allow forgiveness to arise little by little until you feel free.

How did this practice work for you? Were you able to forgive yourself and others? Were you able to imagine that others have forgiven you? Remember, this takes practice and I recommend that you continue to practice until you don't have any charge about forgiving yourself.

ABOUT THE AUTHOR

Dr. Jerome Freedman is a remarkable individual whose life journey spans a diverse tapestry of roles and contributions, each reflecting his unwavering dedication to well-being, mindfulness, and the betterment of our world.

As an accomplished author, Dr. Freedman shares his wisdom and insights through a series of transformative publications, including *Mindfulness Breaks, Stop Cancer in its Tracks*, and *Healing with the Seven Principles of Mindfulness*. These works serve as practical guides for those seeking mindfulness as a path to healing and personal growth.

Jerome's impactful career extends beyond writing. He is a compassionate healthcare mentor, offering invaluable guidance to individuals navigating the complexities of health and healing. His certification as a mindfulness meditation teacher and trauma-sensitive practitioner underscores his commitment to promoting mental and emotional well-being.

A resilient bladder cancer survivor since 1997, Jerome's personal journey has fueled his passion for supporting others facing health challenges. His experiences have imparted profound insights into the resilience of the human spirit.

Rooted in the tradition of Zen Master Thich Nhat Hanh, Jerome is an ordained member of the Order of Interbeing, exemplifying his dedication to mindfulness and compassionate living. His active involvement in various committees within this tradition underscores his commitment to fostering its teachings.

Currently, Jerome imparts his wisdom as a teacher of *Mindfulness in Healing* at the Pine Street Clinic in San Anselmo, California, where he has transitioned to virtual instruction through Zoom. He also shares daily reflections and guidance on his blog, **Meditation Practices**, offering a source of inspiration and mindfulness tools to a global audience.

Jerome's compassion extends to his role as a contributing author of *I Am With You: Love Letters to Cancer Patients*, a heartfelt collection offering support and solace to those navigating the challenges of illness, co-authored with Nancy Novak, PhD, and Barbara K. Richardson.

Beyond his contributions to healthcare and mindfulness, Jerome has made a lasting impact in advocacy. His service on the Board of Directors of the Marin AIDS Project and the Advisory Council of the Institute for Health and Healing between 2007 and 2010 highlights his commitment to community well-being.

In recent years, Jerome has been a tireless advocate for medical research, serving as a patient advocate for the Congressionally Directed Medical Research Programs (CDMRP) and presenting at the 2022 Bladder Cancer Summit. His advocacy has even taken him to the halls of Congress, where he passionately advocates for research funding for the Bladder Cancer Advocacy Network.

Jerome is a dedicated environmental activist and a long-time contributor to the Earth Holder Sangha, the Plum Village climate response community. Through his advocacy for earth protection, he seeks to inspire positive change and stewardship of our planet.

With a Ph.D. in computer science, two master's degrees in physics, and a bachelor's degree in chemical engineering, Jerome bridges the worlds of science and spirituality. His thought-provoking conversation with Dr. Neil deGrasse Tyson on cosmology and Buddhist thought in 2011 exemplifies his ability to explore the intersection of these disciplines.

Jerome is available for consultations, dharma talks, lectures, and days of mindfulness, and you can connect with him via email at jerome [at] mountainsangha [dot] org.

In addition to his written works, Jerome offers a series of *Mindfulness Break Recordings* designed to promote well-being, including Anger Control, Achieve Goals, Sound Sleep, Stress Relief, Reduce Symptoms, and Weight Loss. These resources are available for order on mountainsangha.org/products, providing practical tools for personal transformation.

Jerome Freedman's multifaceted contributions and unwavering commitment to holistic well-being continue to inspire and empower individuals on their own journeys of self-discovery and healing.

www.ingramcontent.com/pod-product-compliance
Lightning Source LLC
Chambersburg PA
CBHW070604010526
44118CB00012B/1445